Study Skills in English

Michael J. Wallace

Don Gres

CAMBRIDGE
UNIVERSITY PRESS

PUBLISHED BY THE PRESS SYNDICATE OF THE UNIVERSITY OF CAMBRIDGE
The Pitt Building, Trumpington Street, Cambridge CB2 1RP, United Kingdom

CAMBRIDGE UNIVERSITY PRESS
The Edinburgh Building, Cambridge CB2 2RU, United Kingdom
40 West 20th Street, New York, NY 10011-4211, USA
10 Stamford Road, Oakleigh, Melbourne 3166, Australia

© Cambridge University Press 1980

First published 1980
Seventeenth printing 1997

Printed in the United Kingdom by
Athenæum Press Ltd, Gateshead, Tyne & Wear

ISBN 0 521 22110 2 Student's Book
ISBN 0 521 22109 9 Tutor's Book
ISBN 0 521 22108 0 Cassette

KY

Contents

This book is dedicated to the memory of my mother.

Acknowledgements

It is impossible for me to list here the names of all the many people who have given me help, encouragement and advice during the writing of this book. I am thinking especially of the hundreds of overseas students who, over the years, have been the target population for the materials now appearing in book form. For their tolerance and constructive criticisms I am very grateful.

I must thank, too, colleagues who have taught this material, and given me the benefit of their comments; especially Pauline Brown, Bill Cousin, Lionel Jackson, Mary Jackson, Alex Peden, Jean Petrie, David Sked, Henry Taylor, Cynthia Watson, and Jim Wight.

Thanks also to: the library staff of Moray House College for their patience and consistent helpfulness; the secretaries in Charteris Secretarial Unit for their cheerful co-operation in typing what must have seemed an endless succession of versions; Alex Brown, Principal Librarian of Moray House College, and Mary Kennaway, Deputy Principal Librarian, for taking the time to read through unit 5 ('Research and using the library'), and giving me the benefit of their comments; Belinda Pyke of the British Council, Edinburgh, for helping me with the references for unit 1 ('Organising your studies'); Ann Brumfit and Keith Morrow for their very helpful comments; the staff of Cambridge University Press, who saw this book through to the publication stage; my wife, Eileen, for her encouragement and moral support.

In spite of all the help I have received, there are shortcomings which no doubt remain, and for these I take full responsibility.

I am grateful to the following for permission to use copyright material:
pp. 10, 22 and 24, Oxford University Press: extracts from Oxford Children's Reference Library, vol. 6 (1967) and vol. 11 (1970); pp. 30 and 32, Macmillan Publishing Co., Inc.: extracts from *Ecology: Science of Survival* by Laurence Pringle (1971); p. 35, George G. Harrap & Co. Ltd: extract from *The Artificial World Around Us* by Lucy Kavaler (1967); pp. 37 and 112, World's Work Ltd: extracts from *Clocks, from Shadow to Atom* by Kathryn

Kilby Borland and Helen Ross Speicher (1970); pp. 39, 43, 44 and 46, Penguin Books Ltd: figures from *Facts in Focus* (fourth edition 1978); p. 40, Routledge & Kegan Paul: table from *The Experience of Higher Education* by Peter Marris (1964); pp. 48 and 49, the Controller of Her Majesty's Stationery Office: figures from *Social Trends* no. 6 (1975) and no. 5 (1974); p. 50, Controller of Her Majesty's Stationery Office: figure from *Flow Charts, Logical Trees and Algorithms for Rules and Regulations* by B. N. Lewis, I. S. Horbin and C. P. Cane (1967); p. 58, Macdonald & Jane's Ltd: extract from *Twentieth Century Discovery* by Isaac Asimov (1971); p. 73, *The Listener*; extract from 'Foundations of Western Values' by James Welch; pp. 86, 87, 89, 90, 93 and 94, Times Newspapers Ltd: extracts from articles in *The Sunday Times*, 11 Sept. 77, 12 Feb. 78, 19 Feb. 78, 14 May 78, 30 April 78, 20 Feb. 77, 11 Sept. 77; p. 107, Methuen & Co. Ltd: extract from *Education and Poverty* by Philip Robinson (1976); p. 108, B. T. Batsford Ltd: extract from *Information in Business and Administrative Systems* by Ronald Stamper (1973); p. 111, George Allen & Unwin Ltd: extract from *Mankind, Nation and the Individual* by Otto Jesperson (1946); p. 112, William Collins Sons & Co. Ltd: extract from *The Earth in Action* by Margaret O. Hyde (1969); p. 123, Worldbook-Childcraft International, Inc.: extract from *The World Book Encyclopedia* vol. 22 (1978); p. 129, *British Book News*; pp. 198 and 199, Longman Group Ltd: extracts from *A Visual Approach to British and American Government* by C. J. Wates and S. T. Miller (1973).

Thanks are also due to the Commonwealth Institute for their help in the taking of the cover photographs.

To the student

This book is for students who have come to Britain, or are shortly about to do so, to study at a college or university.

You will probably find the experience of studying in Britain both enjoyable and rewarding, but you may also find some problems – especially at the beginning of your studies. Some of these problems will be general to all students, and some will be particular to you because you are a foreigner and not a native speaker of English. These problems can be overcome, but they can be very daunting at the beginning.

This book is intended to help you overcome at least some of the difficulties involved in studying in English. In particular, it is designed to answer these questions:

How can I read efficiently?
In your studies you will probably have quite a lot of reading to do. You will want to get it done as quickly and efficiently as possible: after all, you don't have an unlimited amount of time. This topic is covered in unit 2.

What is the best method of taking notes?
Partly this is a personal thing, but there are also some new techniques which have been found useful. In unit 3 you will get a chance to practise these.

How should I prepare myself for seminars and tutorials?
More and more teaching is being done in small groups. This can be a more effective method of learning than the big lecture, but only if the members of the group bring the right attitudes to the small-group sessions, and know what these sessions can, and cannot, do. This topic is dealt with in unit 4.

How do I set about researching a major piece of written work? How do I organise and present it?
You will probably be asked to write an occasional long essay, or write up a major project. This usually involves doing some research, organising your material and presenting it to the best advantage. Since this area may make all the difference between passing and failing a course, three units are devoted to it (units 5, 6 and 7).

I

How should I prepare for examinations?
Usually passing an examination is simply a matter of hard work, but not always: sometimes good candidates do not do themselves full justice, because they neglect a basic aspect of examination strategy. Unit 8 discusses examination strategy, and also deals with certain general study problems that some students have.

In addition to this, unit 1 is designed to help you with some of the more personal and social aspects of being a student in Britain, which can be quite important.

If you work your way through this book, or through the parts of it that are most relevant to your needs, you should be well prepared to play your part in college or university life. You may even find yourself better prepared mentally to overcome your problems than other students who have not thought about, and practised, the skills which lead to successful study.

Unit 1 Organising your studies

There are some people who are natural students. They always do the right thing at the right time, as if by instinct. They are never late with their work, and are always well-prepared for any test that they have to undergo. Unfortunately, this kind of student is very rare. Most of us find ourselves in a state of panic and unpreparedness at some time or other, or even of deep despair of ever being successful in our studies. We think: 'If only I had . . .' – usually when it is too late! This is natural – perhaps even normal – but in most cases it is also avoidable; we recognise this fact when we say: 'If only I had . . .'. Now, at the beginning of your studies in Britain, is a good time to look at your life-style as a student, and ask yourself if it is helping you to succeed, or not.

To help you in this, you will find four self-assessment questionnaires printed below.

For the first three questionnaires you will see that there are three blank columns. Look at the questions and then put a tick ✓ in the 'Yes' or 'No' column, as appropriate. Leave the 'For attention' column blank for the time being.

1 College work

For attention		*Yes*	*No*
	1 Have you got a clear idea in your own mind of the ways in which the course that you are doing will benefit you?		
	2 In general, do you find the subjects that you are doing interesting and stimulating?		
	3 If you had problems with a certain subject, would you discuss them with your tutor?		
	4 Do you miss classes from time to time?		
	5 Are you often late for classes?		
	6 Do you feel that the amount of work you have to do is too much for you?		
	7 Do you hand in work on time?		

3

8 Do you have a system for doing the work that you are given?

9 Do you have a system for keeping notes, handouts etc on the same subject together?

10 Do you take *outline* notes of lectures, discussions, important texts etc?

11 Do you contribute to tutorial discussions?

12 Do you have any kind of cataloguing system for keeping track of the books you read?

2 Private study

For attention   *Yes   No*

1 Do you have a room where you can study privately?

2 Is your private place of study
   a) properly heated?
   b) properly lit?
   (If you have answered 'No' to question 1, leave these blank.)

3 Do you have access to a library or reading room where you can work during your free time?

4 Do you know the opening and closing times of your college/university library?

5 Do you know how the library is organised?

6 Do you know how many hours a week you spend
   a) in classes?
   b) on private study?
   c) on recreation?

7 Have you made a plan of the number of hours per week you will have to spend on
   a) writing essays
   b) revision?
   c) other kinds of private study (e.g. reading)?

3 General way of life

1   Do you have a hobby or recreation which takes your mind off your studies for a while?

2   Do you take part in sport or take other regular exercise?

3   Do you belong to any college/university clubs or societies?

4   Do you get enough sleep (i.e. 7–8 hours per night)?

5   Do you eat a proper balanced diet (especially important if you are looking after yourself)?

6   Do you make lists of things that you have to do, and cross them off each day?

7   Have you got a small notebook in which you you can jot down ideas, book references and so on?

4 Special problems

The problems which we have been looking at apply to all students. There are also other problems which may affect you as a foreign student more severely. This section gives you the opportunity to think about them, and perhaps discuss them. Write down your comments.

1   Do you find it difficult to relate to British students, or to British people generally?
2   (Especially for private, i.e. unsponsored, students): Do you have financial problems in 'making ends meet'?
3   Do you find it difficult to get used to British food?
4   Do you suffer a lot from the cold weather?
5   Do you find difficulty in understanding the books that you have to read?
6   Do you find that it takes you a long time to read books in English?
7   Do you have difficulty in following discussion in tutorials etc?
8   Are you conscious of any problems in writing English?
9   Have you got
   a) a good dictionary?
   b) a good reference grammar of English?

Now compare your answers with those of the average successful student given in the Appendix (p. 191). As you check each questionnaire, put a large X in the space on the left-hand side ('For attention') where your answer is different.

Go over the items labelled X. These items show areas of weakness in you as a student. Some of the weaknesses will be less important than others. For example, it is possible to do well in your studies even if you don't have a private place of study; lack of interest in a subject, however, may be a more serious matter.

When you have finished, discuss your areas of weakness, and also any comments you have written down in answer to questionnaire 4 'Special problems', with your tutor.

You may also find it useful to have a class discussion of some of the problem areas highlighted by these questionnaires, and any others that occur to you.

Need for a personal timetable

One of the things you should know is where your time goes. It is very easy to deceive yourself that you are working harder than you really are. To help you keep track of how you spend your time, you will find a blank timetable on p. 7 opposite, which you can copy to suit your own requirements.

There are two ways you can use the timetable:
a) If you are very conscientious, you can keep an hour-by-hour 'diary' for a week of how you spend your time – travelling, attending classes, meals etc. This will probably be very interesting for you, and you may be surprised at the results.
b) Most people, however, don't have the patience to keep an hour-by-hour account. If you feel this way, you can concentrate on 'study hours', i.e. the number of hours you spend doing all kinds of study (reading, writing essays, etc), outside the time actually spent in class. (You will find more information about 'study hours' in unit 8, pp. 173–4.) Shade in as accurately as you can the time spent on private study.

How you plan to spend your time
You can use a similar timetable to help you plan how you *intend* to spend your time. Again, you can either do this in detail, filling in times for recreation, classes, meals etc, or you can simply concentrate on study hours.

Be realistic – and be fair to yourself. Do not put down a study programme that you cannot hope to achieve. Leave time for recreation, cups of coffee with friends, reading that is not

Diary of a week

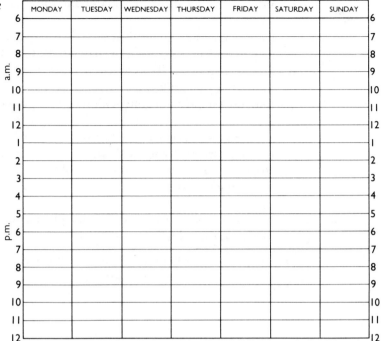

connected with your studies and so on. Over the next week, see how far what you have planned fits in with what you are able to do. This should give you some idea of the time that you really have for study, and what you can reasonably expect to do. Discuss what you have discovered with your tutor.

The student's survival kit

This is a summary of the information you need to survive as a student! Note down the answers to the following questions somewhere where you can easily refer to them again, e.g. in your note-taking file or diary.

1   Who is there in an official position that you can discuss personal problems with?
2   Who can help you with advice on accommodation?
3   Who can help you with general academic problems?
4   List your hobbies and sports.
5   Do you know of teams, clubs etc which exist connected with the hobbies and sports that you are interested in? (Your tutor may be able to advise you on where to find information.)
6   Where would you find details of films, plays, concerts, and other entertainments in your area?

7 Who is your local doctor? (Name and address and phone number.)
8 Do you know of any student service that gives emergency help to students? (Your tutor may be able to help here.)
9 Is there a Students' Representative Council (or something similar) in your college?
10 If so, does it have someone with special responsibility either for
   a) overseas students in general? or
   b) the course that you are doing?
11 What are the hours of your college library
   a) during term-time?
   b) during vacation?
12 Do you know of any other libraries where you can study? When do they close?

If there is any other kind of information you feel you need, discuss it with your tutor and note the details.

Unit 2   Improving your reading efficiency

Reading with a purpose

Before you start reading a book or long article that is connected
with your studies, it is always worthwhile taking a minute or two
to ask yourself *why* you are reading it, and *what* you hope to learn
from it. If you have no clear purpose in reading a text, or if you
are confused about the purpose, the result can be: boredom; lack
of comprehension; misunderstanding; or simply time wasted.
Similarly, when you have finished reading, ask yourself: Have
my purposes in reading been answered? What have I learnt?

Exercise 1

Different purposes require different kinds of reading material.
Suggest the *kind* of reading material which one might use to fulfil
the purposes under A. What do you think of the purposes under
B? In what way are they different from those in A?

Reasons for reading:
A 1 to get a general idea of what a particular subject is all about,
       expressed in language that is not too technical.
    2 to pass the time.
    3 to keep up-to-date with what is happening in the world.
    4 to find some information that might be useful for an
       essay.
    5 to get information about a country one intends to visit.
B 1 because the book is on the course booklist.
    2 to keep up with the other students.

Exercise 2

1 Read the passage on 'Carbon' below (p. 10), with the following purpose: to find out what nylon is made from. Which
   part of the passage satisfies this purpose? Give line numbers.
2 Now look through the passage again with this purpose in
   mind: to find out what we mean by 'Hydrocarbon'. Find the
   information as quickly as you can. Give line numbers.
3 Lastly read it with this purpose: to find out what is 'special'
   about carbon atoms. Give line numbers.

What do you notice about where the information is located in the
text? Are the line numbers the same for questions 1, 2 and 3?

Carbon

Carbon is a very special material, and there are atoms of it in
many things: for instance the 'lead' of a pencil is made of
carbon, coal is made of carbon, and so are diamonds. A
number of other things such as wood, plants, and oil are made
very largely of carbon, but have other substances as well. The   5
molecules which make up our bodies depend on carbon.
  Carbon atoms are so special because they have the property
of joining together into molecules in different ways. For
instance, the atoms of coal and diamonds are joined together to
make crystals, but each in its own pattern, and consequently   10
from carbon atoms come two things so different to look at. A
pencil 'lead' is also carbon, but here the atoms are arranged not
in crystals but in flat sheets, far too small, of course, to see.
When we press a pencil onto paper, the paper pulls some of the
sheets of atoms away, and these make the pencil marks. Paper   15
may feel smooth, but it is rough enough to slide off some sheets
of atoms. If you try to write on glass and cellophane, your
pencil leaves no marks, for these are too smooth to pull the
sheets away from the pencil 'lead'.
  Besides forming into crystals and making sheets, carbon   20
atoms can also form into long series of atoms, like chains. No
other substance can do this so well. Each chain of carbon atoms
can also have other substances attached to the links of the
carbon chain. If the carbon chain has hydrogen atoms joined
on to it, we have what scientists call a 'hydrocarbon'.   25
Hydrocarbons give us molecules of oil, petrol, paraffin, tar, and
natural gas, like that found under the North Sea.
  Scientists have discovered that carbon chains can be very
long, and can contain thousands of both carbon and other
atoms. These long carbon chains are single molecules, but   30
much more complicated than the single molecules of water,
for instance, which are made of only three atoms (one of
oxygen and two of hydrogen). These are the molecules of very
complicated substances such as plastics, and living things such
as our bodies, plants, and many kinds of food. The long chain   35
of carbon and other atoms can be coiled up in different and
very complicated ways. They can also be arranged in rings.
The difference between different kinds of oils, such as petrol
and paraffin, depends on the way in which the atoms are
arranged in the molecules. The chemist can make petrol or   40
paraffin from the oil out of an oil-well by heating it enough to
change the pattern of the atoms in its molecules.
  The chemist today has found out how to make new
substances by heating materials made of hydrocarbon chains,
such as oil or coal, in giant pressure cookers and mixing with   45

them other chemicals. When very hot indeed, the atoms of the
other chemicals fit into the hydrocarbon chain and combine to
make molecules of a new pattern. The result of this may be a
plastic for making cups or washing-up bowls, or an artificial
fibre for making clothes. Nylon, for example, is a man-made   50
fibre with molecules made out of carbon chains in which atoms
of nitrogen, hydrogen, and oxygen fit in a particular
arrangement. Milk contains carbon chains, and the chemist can
extract these and re-form them into a plastic for making solid
things such as buttons and door handles.   55
    The carbon chains in living things are even more
complicated than those in oils, plastics, or artificial fibres, and
may contain hundreds of thousands of atoms; there is often
more than one chain in each molecule, and these may be
twisted together like ropes or bundles. It is a difficult problem   60
for the scientist to unravel these complicated molecules, and
therefore, although he can make an artificial fibre, he has not
yet been able to fit the molecules together to make a living
plant or animal.

(From *A Book of Science* by Colin Ronan)

The fact is that having a definite purpose in mind means that
some parts of what you read will probably not be relevant – these
parts can be missed out or skimmed over very quickly. Other
parts will be highly relevant and have to be studied in detail. Of
course, it is quite possible that the information you are looking
for may not be in the text after all – in which case, the sooner you
find this fact out, the less time you will waste.

    You should therefore *read actively*, i.e. with a clear purpose or
with certain questions in mind. To read actively often means to
read selectively, i.e. concentrating on what is relevant to your
purpose. In the next few sections we shall discuss some other
techniques to help bring about active reading.

Using the title

Sometimes, when you are reading through a bibliography, you
have to make a decision, on the basis of the title alone, as to
whether the book or article in question is going to be relevant to
you. Usually, the titles of academic books and articles are factual
and informative: they can almost be taken as very brief
summaries of the contents of the text. So, when you are
considering the title of a book or article, you have to ask yourself
two questions:
1 Is this text relevant (or might it be relevant) to my purpose?
2 If it is relevant, what sort of question do I expect it to answer?

What do I expect to learn from it? (These questions that you ask yourself *before* you read a text are called 'anticipation questions'.)

Exercise 3

Below are five titles taken from magazines on Geography. Choose *three* of the titles and, for each title, write down *two* anticipation questions which you think the article might answer.

1 'Italian migration to Great Britain' (by R. King, *Geography*, vol. 62, part 3, July 1977)
2 'Water in Kuwait' [NB Kuwait is an arid (dry) Middle Eastern Country] (by P. Beaumont, *Geography*, vol. 62, part 3, July 1977)
3 'Life in India behind the veil' (by Doranne Wilson Jacobson, *National Geographic*, vol. 152, no. 2, August 1977. Cover title)
4 'First colony in Space' (by Isaac Asimov, *National Geographic*, vol. 150, no. 1, July 1976. Cover title)
5 'Solar energy, the ultimate powerhouse' (by John L. Wilhelm, *National Geographic*, vol. 149, no. 3, March 1976)

Now check your questions with the outlines of the articles in the Appendix, p. 191. How good are you at forming 'anticipation questions'?

Exercise 4

The aim of this exercise is the same as the previous one – to show how you can have an active approach to reading by asking yourself questions before you start reading.

The passage which follows is entitled 'Aspects of the reading process and reading efficiency'. Can you suggest *two* questions which you might reasonably expect the chapter to cover?

Read the passage and see if your questions are answered!

Aspects of the reading process and reading efficiency

What actually happens when we read? Some people think that we read one word at a time, understand it and then go on to the next. Other people think that our eyes smoothly glide over each line from left to right, then back to the beginning of the next line, and so on. In fact, the physical process of reading usually doesn't work in either of those ways.

Suppose you do this experiment with a friend. Get hold of a book with a large page size and lines that go right across the page. Get your friend to hold the book up and to read it with the top of the book just below his eye level. This means that you can watch the movement of his eyes as he reads the page. If you do this, you will see that your friend's eyes do not make a continuous forward sweep. Instead they progress by little 'jumps', moving, then stopping, as they progress along the line. This kind of jumping movement is called a *saccadic* movement.

There has to be this starting and stopping movement because the eye can see only when it is *still*, i.e. motionless. Every time the eye pauses it sees a phrase or even a sentence, then jumps to the next part of the line, and so on.

So you may have read the last sentence like this:

Every time/the eye pauses/
it sees a phrase/or even a sentence,/then jumps/to the next part/of the line,/
and so on./

There is another interesting fact about eye movement. If you record the eye movements of someone who is reading, you will notice that, from time to time, the reader goes back and looks again at something he has read before; in other words, he *regresses* to an earlier part of the text, probably because he realises he is not understanding the passage properly. Then he comes back to where he left off and continues reading. At one time, it was thought that regression was a fault, but it is in fact a very necessary activity in efficient reading.

There are several different kinds of faults in reading, which are usually more exaggerated with foreign learners. The most common one is that most people read more slowly than they should. There is no rate at which people ought to read, of course: it depends on your purpose in reading, how difficult the language is, how unfamiliar the material and so on. But most people read everything at the same slow speed, and do not seem to realise that they can read faster or slower as required. Other people say the words to themselves, or move their lips – these habits slow the reader down to something near speaking speed, which is, of course, much slower than reading speed. Another habit which can slow you down is following the line with your finger, or with a pen.

If you want to be able to read faster, the secret is simply to practise under timed conditions. This means that you should give yourself a certain amount of time to read with understanding, then check your time when you have finished. Students who have practised fast reading even for only an hour a week, have shown average improvements of over 50% over a term of ten weeks' duration. Reading fast does not necessarily mean reading with less comprehension – in fact, usually students show a small increase in comprehension as well as a dramatic increase in speed.

Did you get the answer to your questions? In a sense it doesn't matter if you didn't, because at least you were *reading actively*, not just letting the author's meaning 'wash over you'.

For the final part of this exercise, write down two questions which you did *not* ask yourself, but which you now know can be answered from the passage. (See if you can do this without checking back to the passage.)

Surveying a book

Another, more reliable, way of building up anticipation, so that you can ask yourself the right kinds of questions, is by *surveying* the text. The exercises which follow practise various surveying techniques.

Too many students read books passively and without judgement: they simply start at page 1 and read through to the end. Think of the book as a *learning tool* to help you master your subject and ask yourself: If you required a tool to do some job would you cheerfully
– choose any old tool whether it was a hammer, chisel etc?
– use a tool that was old and covered in rust?
– use a tool that was damaged or faulty?
Apply the same standards to books and ask yourself
– is it relevant to the topic I am interested in?
– is all of it relevant or only a part? Which part?
– is it by a reputable writer, whose judgement can be trusted? (Your tutor may have to help you with this.)
– is it out-of-date?
– is it too far above or too far below the level I am studying at?
There may also be other factors: it may be too long for you to read right through, and so on.

Exercise 5

Parts of the book which may help you to answer the sort of questions we have been asking are
1 the publisher's *blurb* (i.e. the publisher's description of what the book is about – usually to be found on the book-jacket).
2 *reviewer's comments* (often also found quoted on the book-jacket: but remember only the *good* reviews will be quoted!)
3 the *foreword* or *preface*.
4 the *contents page*.
5 the *index*.
6 the *printing history* (i.e. when the book was first published, reprinted, new edition issued – usually printed on one of the early pages).

Some of this information for a book called *An Introduction to Sociology* by J. E. Goldthorpe is printed below (pp. 15–19). Use it to answer the following questions:
1 What is the author's academic position? Is his position relevant to the subject matter of the book?
2 When was the book first published? Has anything been done to bring it up to date since then?

3 What audience was the book written for? Has the author any experience, do you think, of knowing the needs of that audience?

4 Apart from what the publisher says, is there any other evidence that the book is a good one?

5 Based on the evidence that you have, which of the following would you say are especial strengths of the book (choose three):

a) simply written
b) extremely comprehensive
c) short
d) written with authority
e) written for advanced students

6 If you were interested in the differences between the class–structure of traditional societies and modern societies, which chapter would you look for the answer in? (You might check the index first, of course.)

Extracts from J. E. Goldthorpe:
An Introduction to Sociology

i) *From the blurb*

This has proved a good introduction to what sociology is and what kinds of information and useful knowledge the practice of this discipline provides. In discussing family structure, the relation between the economy and society and social class, the author uses appropriate examples of African experience.

The new edition has up-dated all the minor terms such as names of countries, and the suggestions for further reading. The treatment of the family, marriage and kinship has been extended by a discussion of the distinction between exogamy and the incest prohibition, and by new material on the family in industrializing societies. The chapter on religion now includes a section about denominationalism and the chapter on social control compares positive and negative sanctions in society. The characterization of culture has been defined more precisely, and has involved a re-working of the author's approach to major institutional areas. The most significant change is the author's recognition of sociology's scientific status, and a new section is devoted to this; he contrasts the ideas on the humanities side with the science of animal behaviour and comments on the special position in which this dichotomy places the social sciences.

*The author is Senior Lecturer in Sociology
University of Leeds*

ii) *From the blurb*

Some comments on the first edition:

' . . . a thoroughly sound and authoritative introduction to sociology written with a simple
directness and clarity that is difficult in any
subject and rare indeed in sociology.'
The Times Educational Supplement

' . . . extremely practical for the specific audience
for which it was intended and it may help to
enrich African sociology. Indeed, even mature
scholars can profit from Godthorpe's informed
but modest evaluation of the place of sociology
in a rapidly changing world.'
American Sociological Review

' . . . commendable for straightforward con-
veyance of ideas and information and general
perspicuity . . . Another merit is its smooth combination of sociological and socio-anthropo-
logical methods and literature.'
Sociology

'A very useful, short introduction to the discip-
lines of Sociology and Social Anthropology.
This book is certainly to be recommended to
first year students in African universities, and it
has been expressly written for them—to stimulate
them "to be the sociologists of the new Africa".'
The Teacher, Uganda

AUTHOR'S PREFACE

TO THE SECOND EDITION

I was honoured and delighted when in 1964 the Syndics of the Cambridge University Press asked me to write a textbook of sociology specially for students in the universities of Africa. Although there is no lack of introductions to sociology, most are written for students living in Europe and America and unfamiliar with the societies of the developing countries. The Syndics' far-sighted perception at that time of the need for a book written, so to speak, the other way round —beginning with the perspectives of an emergent Africa and leading on to a wider reality, including that of the affluent industrial societies — has been abundantly justified, to such an extent that there is now a need for a second edition. After writing a book of this kind, it is natural that an author should come to have second thoughts about some of the things he said in it. Some controversies that appeared central and perennial in 1966, when most of this book was first written, now no longer seem so; some illustrative examples that then seemed appropriate now appear ill-chosen; and some recent discoveries have made it necessary to modify the approach to important areas of the subject. It is good to have the opportunity to carry out a full revision in the light of scholarly reviews of the first edition as well as of my subsequent reading, thought, and discussion.

I am grateful for the encouragement successively of Professor Eugene Grebenik in writing the book in the first place, and of Professor Zygmunt Bauman in revising it. Academic authorship depends heavily on the kindly help of library staff and secretaries, which I have had in full measure at the University of Leeds. I am grateful for the friendly help of the staff of the Cambridge University Press at all stages. Most important of all, it is by the interchange of ideas that we are kept intellectually alive, and for that I must thank colleagues and students here and in Africa.

J. E. G.

May 1973

CONTENTS

Published by the Syndics of the Cambridge University Press
The Pitt Building, Trumpington Street, Cambridge CB2 1RP
Bentley House, 200 Euston Road, London NW1˙2DB
32 East 57th Street, New York, NY 10022, USA
296 Beaconsfield Parade, Middle Park, Melbourne 3206, Australia

© Cambridge University Press 1968, 1974

Library of Congress catalogue card number: 73–83107

ISBNs: Second edition 0 521 20338 4 hard covers   0 521 09826 2 paperback
(First edition 0 521 07110 0 hard covers   0 521 09547 6 paperback)

First published 1968
Reprinted 1969 1971
Second edition 1974
Reprinted 1975 1976 1978

Photoset and printed in
Malta by Interprint (Malta) Ltd

Exercise 6

In this exercise, we shall see what kind of information can be
found in an index. On p. 20 below you will find a page from the
index of *An Introduction to Sociology*. Use it to answer the
following questions:

1 Which of the following topics does the author deal with *at
   length*, and which seem to be covered *briefly*?
   a) libraries
   b) indirect rule
   c) law
   d) Islam
   e) kinship
2 An author may make a passing reference to a topic, or he may
   treat it extensively. Where in the book (which pages) would
   you expect to find the most extensive account of:
   a) legitimacy
   b) kinship
   c) lineage
   d) division of labour

218   *Index*

We have seen some ways in which you can do a quick survey of a book. Other parts of a book worth looking at are *the first chapter* and *the last chapter*.

In the first chapter, the writer sometimes outlines what topics he is going to deal with in the book (if he hasn't already done so in a preface or foreword). The last chapter is often very good for survey purposes, because there the writer may summarise his main arguments and list his conclusions. So make a habit of looking at the *last* chapter *first*!

Surveying a chapter using first lines of paragraphs

Just as it is a good idea to survey a book, the same thing applies to a chapter or larger passage in a book. It is obvious that a chapter which deals with a topic we are very familar with should be quicker to read and must be easier to understand. But what if the topic is unfamiliar? By quickly surveying the chapter, we can make ourselves familiar with its general drift. This means that we can then read it more efficiently. The next five exercises show some ways of surveying a chapter.

Exercise 7

The chapters in exercises 7 and 9 come from a standard work of reference for young people. This book is concerned with explaining clearly various aspects of earth-science. The first chapter is entitled 'The surface of the earth'. Before the chapter begins, you will see one-sentence summaries of what the chapter is all about. Read through them. Then survey the chapter *by reading the first sentence in each paragraph only*. To help you these sentences have been printed *in italics*. Then, go back to the summaries; which is the correct one?

Summary 1. This chapter is mainly about all the different races of people we find on the surface of the earth.
Summary 2. This chapter is mainly about the different uses that the surface of the earth can be put to.
Summary 3. This chapter is mainly about various ways in which rocks on the earth's surface are broken up by natural forces.
Summary 4. This chapter is mainly about how slowly the earth's surface is changing.

The surface of the earth

To most of us the face of the earth – with its mountains, rivers, plains, and seas – does not seem to change at all. But if we happen to live in certain places, perhaps near an active volcano, or a powerful, swift-flowing river, or on the coast, we may be able to see some change taking place – the river changing its course, or the sea wearing down parts of the cliffs. In fact, these changes are going on all the time, but usually so slowly that there is hardly anything that can be measured in a man's lifetime. But a man's lifetime is so short that it hardly counts in the history of the earth. If a valley becomes deeper by only one inch each 100 years, it will have deepened by about 500 feet in 500,000 years, and even that is only a comparatively short time in the whole life of the earth.

Running water, glaciers, the wind, the waves and currents of the seas, heat and cold, and plants have all been working together for millions of years changing the face of the earth. Changes begin with the breaking up of rock into pieces that can be moved. Rock becomes broken up either by force of one kind or another, or by being rotted by chemicals dissolved in rain-water, or in streams and rivers. When rock has been cracked or broken by force it is more easily rotted by chemical action, and rock that has been rotted is more easily broken by force.

All rocks cannot be broken equally easily by force since they are made of different materials and in different ways. Some began to break up deep underground: they were cracked and splintered as they cooled or as they were twisted and pushed by the forces which shaped the mountains. Those that were made in layers break most easily between the layers where they are weakest. Natural forces that break up rock masses use such cracks and lines of weakness.

Tiny plants may root themselves in the cracks of rocks, and as they grow, their roots grow too and push and push, opening the crack, and in time even splitting the rock. Water and frost are powerful rock splitters. Water may freeze in a crack and, as water expands when it turns into ice, the ice presses on the crack and makes it bigger. Most swift-flowing streams carry downstream rocks and boulders, and as these are rolled and swung along by the water, they strike the rock in the stream banks and bed and break off pieces. Forest fires often weaken and crack rock, and rock can also be shattered by lightning.

These many ways of breaking up rock go on everywhere in the world. They work most quickly in places where the rocks have cracks and weaknesses, where there are many trees and plants with strong, pushing roots, and in cold climates where there is frequent freezing and thawing.

Rocks are broken up by chemical action fastest in rainy places in hot climates, for the chemicals dissolve in rain-water and they act more quickly in warm weather. Rocks made of hard material closely packed do not break up so easily since there are no cracks through which water can enter; but porous rocks, which allow water to pass through, break up more easily.

Breaking up of rocks by chemical action goes on underground as well as on the surface of the earth. Great tunnels, galleries, and caves have been worn away in limestone rocks by underground water, and sometimes the roofs of these tunnels have fallen in, making gorges.

(From *The Earth* by Jean Petrie)

Exercise 8

Now check your answer to exercise 7 by reading *all* of the passage through again quickly. Time yourself and check your reading speed against the table in the Appendix, p. 193. Note down:
starting time
finishing time
reading time (mins and secs, to the nearest 10 secs)
reading speed

Did you get it right? You should have found that your survey helped you to read the complete chapter more efficiently.

Exercise 9

This exercise and the next one are similar to exercises 7 and 8. This time the chapter heading is 'Terrible winds'. Which *two* of the following four topics are dealt with *at greatest length* in the chapter?
a) Gales
b) Thunderstorms
c) Tornadoes
d) Hurricanes

Terrible winds

Sometimes winds move in violent storms which do a great deal of damage and are so strong that they are terrifying. These storms happen when a mass of hot air meets a mass of cold air.

Winds are measured by the speed per hour which they travel. They are called gales when they are strong enough to uproot trees and blow down chimneys, and at sea to whip up high waves with long crests that curl over and break in great patches of foam. Gale-force winds have a speed of over 39 miles per hour, and often the strongest gusts reach a speed of 80 to 100 m.p.h. In Britain, gales are sometimes part of the changing weather that we get when air of very low pressure, called a deep depression, moves eastwards from the north Atlantic Ocean.

Thunderstorms happen when hot, damp air rises from the ground and meets cold air. As it mixes with colder air, there are very violent upcurrents and down currents and swirling eddies of air, and great clouds form. Air-pilots caught in thunderclouds have described how they have met gusts so strong that their aircraft have been hurled about and severely damaged. The lightning flashes which accompany thunderstorms are enormous sparks caused by electric charges in the air. They have such great heat that the air they touch expands violently, making the sound we call thunder.

Gales and thunderstorms happen all over the world. Tornadoes, waterspouts and hurricanes happen only in certain areas.

Tornadoes happen in the tropics over land, especially over the southern states of the U.S.A., and also over south-eastern Australia and north-west India. A tornado is a very violent windstorm, in which the air whirls rapidly upwards in a greyish funnel-shaped cloud, with its tip near the ground. It twists and sways in the sky like a diving thing and moves in a straight line over the countryside at about 6 to 30 m.p.h. No-one knows exactly what starts a tornado, but it certainly happens when extremely hot, moist air meets cold, dry air. When two kinds of air try to pass each other they get locked together, and the hot air spirals upwards more and more quickly until it may be whirling round at between 400 and 500 m.p.h.

Tornadoes do a vast amount of damage, even though they seldom last for more than an hour or two. The speed of the whirling air makes quite small things such as grains of sand into dangerous weapons. Once in America a corn cob picked up by a tornado was shot through a horse's skull and killed the horse. The hot air spiralling upwards sucks up everything in its path, rather as a vacuum cleaner does. Tornadoes have been known to tear steel bridges from their foundations, to uproot large trees, and to lift trains off their lines. People and animals have been lifted and carried some distance; a horse, for example, was once picked up, carried 2 miles, and put down again unhurt. Queer things happen, such as corks flying out of bottles and closed boxes and houses exploding as the air within them rushes out with great violence.

A waterspout is a tornado that happens over sea. The whirling air sucks up water, and the waterspout moves along with a hissing, roaring, crashing noise. Sometimes tiny fishes are caught up, and their scales make the whirling column sparkle. When a waterspout passes from sea to land it becomes a tornado.

Hurricanes are even more terrible than tornadoes. Nowhere are they more terrible and more frequent than in the West Indies, and the name 'hurricane' comes from the name of the West Indian god of storms, Hunraken. They are called tropical cyclones in India, typhoons in China and Japan, and willy-willies in northern Australia.

Hurricanes begin over tropical oceans in late summer. Hot, moist air rises as if in a chimney, perhaps over a tropical islet. It gets pulled by the turning of the Earth into a whirling movement, faster and faster until it is like an enormous thick gramophone record of air whirling madly round as it moves across the sea at between 12 and 24 m.p.h. It may be anything between 50 and 500 miles across, and it may be whirling round at speeds of up to 250 m.p.h. Many hurricanes never reach land but die out over the tropical oceans, having perhaps moved as much as 1,800 miles during their life of 9 to 25 days. Those that reach land die swiftly, for they need the heat and moisture of ocean air. But before dying they cause terrible destruction. They flatten trees and buildings, flood everything with the torrential rain they bring with them, and sometimes create enormous waves which sweep inland over sea walls and harbours. In a terrible typhoon in Japan in 1934, over 4,000 people were killed and ships were lifted over sea walls into the streets.

Now people usually get warning by wireless that a hurricane is moving in their direction, and they can take refuge from it in specially built shelters. Hurricanes are given names, always feminine ones such as Betsy or

Alice. The first of the season is given a name beginning with 'A', the second with 'B', and so on. Hurricanes in some years have reached Janey or Katy.

(From *The Earth* by Jean Petrie)

Exercise 10

Now check if your answer to exercise 9 was correct by reading quickly through the passage. Time yourself and check your reading speed against the table in the Appendix p. 193. Note down:
starting time
finishing time
reading speed against the table in the Appendix, p. 193. Note reading speed

Surveying a chapter using first and last paragraphs

Sometimes the first or last paragraph of a chapter may have special significance. The writer may state in the first paragraph what he intends to write about; or he may summarise what he has been saying in the last paragraph. This is illustrated in the next exercise.

Exercise 11

The next passage is entitled 'Malaria – a new threat'. Immediately you will ask yourself the question: Why is malaria called a *new* threat? It has been a threat to man for thousands of years. Have you any ideas to explain the title? Think about it.
Survey. Quickly read the *first sentence* of each paragraph and *all* of the last paragraph. Then see if you can answer this question:
Why does the writer call malaria a *new* threat?
Read. Now read quickly through the whole passage, and see whether you can answer the questions which come after it. Time yourself.
Note your starting time (for reading *only*).

Malaria – a new threat

Malaria has been the scourge of humanity since the earliest times, and there are ominous signs that it is fighting back against Modern Science. The first great breakthrough in the treatment of malaria was the discovery by Sir Ronald Ross that the disease was transmitted by the female *Anopheles* mosquito. Giovanni Grassi worked out the life cycle of the human malaria parasite.

25

With the connection between malaria and the mosquito clearly established, steps could be taken to fight the disease.

One method was to attack the breeding places of the mosquito. It was known that mosquitoes laid their eggs in water. So, in malaria infested areas work was started on draining marshes, stagnant pools, and trying to ensure generally that there were no areas of water where mosquitoes could breed. Where areas of still water could not be drained, they were sometimes covered with oil or detergent, which made them unusable by the mosquitoes.

One of the more ingenious modern methods of preventing mosquitoes from multiplying is to introduce a different variety of mosquito into an area: when the two varieties mate, the females are infertile. This kind of 'biological engineering' has had some limited success in the field, but it is not always possible to reproduce laboratory conditions in real life. Since there are over 2,600 different kinds of mosquitoes, the research problems are enormous.

The most obvious and easiest method of prevention is to use wire screens and mosquito netting to prevent people being bitten. But this is obviously not of much use in poor areas, or when people are travelling about.

A more flexible method is to take protective drugs such as quinine. This drug was at one time extremely widely used, but during the Second World War most of the supply areas fell to the Japanese and alternative methods had to be found in the West. These drugs proved to be more effective in many ways, and the use of quinine tailed away. Recently, however, there have been indications that certain varieties of malaria germs are becoming resistant to the more modern drugs, and quinine is coming into use once more.

At one time, it seemed that insecticides, especially DDT, might wipe out malaria completely. One of the most successful DDT campaigns was carried out in India. In 1952, at the beginning of the campaign, seventy-five million Indians a year suffered from malaria. By 1965, the spraying of DDT had reduced the number of cases to 100,000.

However, as with the malaria germ and preventive drugs, there is evidence that mosquitoes are developing resistance to DDT. One of the reasons for this has been the initial success of the operation. People became careless. Also, owing to the fuel crisis, poorer countries found it impossible to maintain the eradication programme. The situation now is that malaria is staging a comeback, and there are new breeds which are resistant to DDT.

So we see that there are various methods of fighting malaria. They involve: preventing mosquitoes from breeding; preventing mosquitoes from having the opportunity to bite people; using protective drugs, and using insecticides. Dangerous new developments are that some malaria germs are developing a resistance to modern drugs, and the mosquitoes themselves are becoming resistant to insecticides.

Note your finishing time, reading time and reading speed. Check your reading speed against the table in the Appendix, p. 193.

Answer these questions as quickly as you can. If you remember the answer write it straight down. If you can't remember, find it quickly. (You can answer in a word or phrase.)

1   What *two* ways have been tried to prevent the mosquitoes from using their breeding grounds?
2   What ingenious modern method of 'biological engineering' has been used against the mosquito?
3   What *three* other methods against malaria are mentioned?
4   Which *two* methods are not as effective as they used to be?

Check your answers in the Appendix, p. 192.

Scanning

We have spoken about *surveying* a book or a chapter, to get a general idea of what it is all about. We are now going to look at the technique of *scanning*. When we are scanning a text we are looking for specific information which we know, or suspect, is there.

Both surveying and scanning are forms of *skimming*, by which we mean that you don't read every word. So we have:

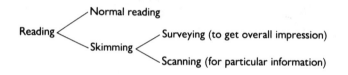

When you are scanning a book for specific information you will sometimes get help from the index, or the list of contents, which are there for that very purpose. With a shorter text you may have less help.

Exercise 12

Here is a simple scanning exercise, but you must do it *quickly*. In each line of words below, one word is printed on the left hand side of the vertical dividing line, and the same word is repeated on the right hand side. Your task is to scan for the repeated word and *underline* it. The first one is done for you. You have *15 seconds* to finish the exercise.

1   newspaper| journal periodical magazine <u>newspaper</u> review bulletin
2   geology| geometry psychology physics logic geography geology
3   anarchism| socialism conservatism Marxism liberalism anarchism capitalism

27

4 plumber| carpenter stonemason plumber glazier
   welder miller
5 sheikh| king shah emperor prince czar sheikh
6 astronomy| astrology astrophysics cosmology
   astronomy astronomer meteorologist
7 linen| cotton linen muslin denim chiffon satin
8 sapphire| diamond ruby sapphire emerald jade
   topaz
9 cobra| cobra adder mamba boa python viper
10 Indian| Iranian Icelandic Iraqui Irish Italian Indian

Exercise 13

Another simple exercise, to be done quickly. It is concerned with
using the scanning technique to get information quickly from an
index. We shall use the index printed on p. 20 above. Keeping
one finger on p. 20 and one on this page, quickly check up the
page references for the following topics. (This exercise should not
take more than 90 seconds.)

leadership	Janowitz, M.
libraries	inequality
household	Kariba
Ivory Coast	

Multiple reading skills (including organisation analysis): practice

There is one technique which helps us all the time that we are
reading, but especially when scanning. It is an awareness of the
organisation of the text. If you look back at the passage in exercise
11 ('Malaria – a new threat') you will see that it has roughly the
kind of organisation shown in the diagram opposite.

There are hundreds of different types of organisation in texts.
For example, in a scientific text one often finds this type of
organisation:

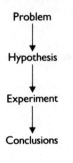

Problem

Hypothesis

Experiment

Conclusions

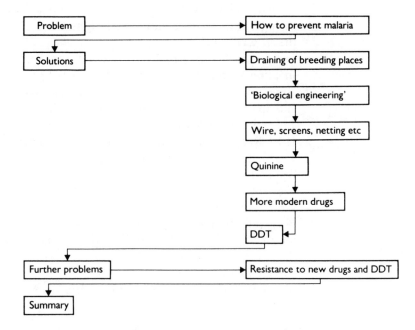

Analysis of text organisation

The simplest type of organisation is *chronological* (i.e. things stated one after another in the order that they happened).

If you know the organisation of a text, you have a better idea of where to find the information you need.

Another advantage of being aware of text organisation is that it makes it much easier to write a *summary*. Being able to summarise, i.e. extract the relevant main ideas from a book, discussion, lecture, etc, is probably one of the most valuable skills you can have as a student. What goes into your summary will often depend on your *purpose* in reading the text: what is relevant to one student may not be relevant to another. The length of your summary will depend on how much detail you want to go into, but obviously summaries should be kept as brief as possible. In the exercises which follow you will be asked to make written summaries as well as diagrams of text organisation – but remember that a diagram may often be the best kind of summary, and easier to memorise, too.

Exercise 14

In this exercise, and the three exercises following, you will have a chance to practise several of the skills we have been discussing.

1 *Using the title.* The next passage is entitled 'Ecosystems' and is from a book called *Ecology – Science of Survival* by Laurence Pringle. Does the title mean anything to you? (Don't worry if the answer is 'No'!)

2 *Survey.* Survey the passage in the usual way, i.e. by reading the first line of each paragraph and all of the last paragraph.

3 *Anticipation.* You should now be able to ask yourself some anticipation questions. Think of *three* anticipation questions and write them down.

4 *Read.* Read the passage through quickly. Don't forget to time yourself. Check your reading speed against the table in the Appendix, p. 193.

5 Can you now answer the anticipation questions? If you can, write down the answers.
Now refer back to the passage and check your answers.

6 *Organisation.* Draw a diagram to represent the organisation of the passage. (You will probably have to refer back to the passage in order to do this.)

7 *Summary.* Use the diagram to write a brief summary of the main points of the passage.

Note your starting time.

Ecosystems

Any ecosystem is made up of two parts: nonliving (the physical environment) and living (the biological community). The nonliving environment usually includes energy from the sun, temperature, water, gases in the air, wind, soils, and the rocks beneath them, and the topography, or shape of the land. These nonliving parts of the ecosystem determine the kinds of life that exist in an ecosystem and they also affect each other.

The world's deserts, for example, occur where the annual rainfall is ten inches or less. This lack of rain is sometimes caused by topography. Along the west coast of North America, winds carry water vapor inland from the Pacific Ocean. The air is forced to rise as it hits the coastal mountain ranges. As it rises it cools and the water vapor in the air falls as rain or snow on the seaward side of the mountains. As a result, there is little rainfall on the other side. This is called the rain shadow effect.

In the Cascade Mountains of Washington, the annual precipitation may reach a hundred inches. Beyond the Cascades, in the Columbia River Valley, the annual rainfall is about nine inches. So the topography has a tremendous influence on the amount of water that falls on the land. This, in turn, affects the plant and animal life. The rain rich western slopes of the Cascades are covered with dense forest. In the rain shadow on the other side of the mountain range, only sagebrush, bunch grasses, and other desert plants grow.

The living parts of an ecosystem often affect the nonliving parts. When rain falls on a forest, the tree branches and leaves help break the force of the drops. Layers of dead leaves on the forest floor soak up water and prevent the drops from washing soil away. Little water runs off the land. So the living trees help maintain the soil on which they depend. In fact, the trees add to the soil, since the leaves that fall to the forest floor eventually decay and become part of the soil itself.

Soils offer the best example of how nonliving and living parts of an ecosystem affect each other. Soil is made up mostly of grains of minerals, such as silica and clay, that are freed as rocks slowly break down. Spaces between the mineral particles are filled with air or water. Roots reach down into the soil, changing it physically (by loosening packed particles) and chemically (by withdrawing minerals). Dead parts of plants and animals are brought deeper into the soil by earthworms and other soil animals. Thousands of organisms live in a handful of soil. Most of them are too small to be seen, but they all affect the soil by taking minerals from it and adding wastes and their dead bodies to it. Soils are of special interest to ecologists because the lives of nearly all land organisms, including humans, depend so much on them.

As ecologists study ecosystems, they often turn to the science of meteorology for information. Does the annual rainfall come mostly in one season, or is it spread evenly over the year? How much does the temperature vary between day and night, and through the year? Finding answers to such questions is important because the climate of an area has a tremendous effect on its plant and animal life. To learn more about the living parts of an ecosystem, you might visit a small pond. To get there, you will probably have to hike through a field or forest. You may cross a stream that flows into the pond, or another that flows out. Clearly, the pond must be affected by other ecosystems, and the pond must affect them.

A pond ecosystem usually contains all of the nonliving factors mentioned above. The sun provides the energy of life. The climate determines how much rain falls in the area, the length of the growing season for plants, and whether the pond is covered with ice in winter. These factors can have a great effect on the life that the pond supports. The underlying rocks and soils affect the chemistry of the water, which in turn helps determine what kinds of plants and animals live in the water. And the life of the pond affects the nonliving environment: when plants and animals die, their remains settle to the bottom and decay there, adding to the bottom muck and making the pond more shallow.

(From *Ecology: Science of Survival* by Laurence Pringle)

Note your finishing time, reading time and reading speed. Check you reading speed against the table in the Appendix, p. 193.

Exercise 15

1 *Using the title.* The next passage is also from Laurence Pringle's *Ecology – Science of Survival* and is entitled 'Predators, parasites

and other relationships'. Does the title bring any ideas to your mind?

2 *Survey.* Survey the passage in the usual way.

3 *Anticipation.* You should now be able to ask yourself some anticipation questions. Think of *three* anticipation questions and write them down.

4 *Read.* Read the passage quickly. Don't forget to time yourself. Check your reading speed against the table in the Appendix, p. 193.

5 Can you now answer the anticipation questions? Write down the answers. Now refer back to the passage and check your answers.

6 *Organisation.* Draw a diagram to represent the organisation of the passage. (Remember that you will probably have to refer back to the passage in order to do this.)

7 *Summary.* Use the diagram to write a brief summary of the main points of the passage.

Note your starting time.

Predators, parasites and other relationships

The living things in an ecosystem affect each other in many ways. The consumers that kill other animals for food are called *predators*. The word predator usually brings to mind pictures of lions and wolves, but such creatures as robins, frogs, and humans are also predators. Some predators, carnivores such as lions, depend entirely on animals they kill, while many others, such as foxes and humans, eat plant food too.

Some people think of predators as 'bad', though humans themselves are the greatest predators the world has known. Sometimes individual predators do prey upon farm animals, and these individuals have to be controlled. Too often, however, people try to wipe out entire populations of predators, with the mistaken idea that they are doing good.

People usually believe that predators have an easy time of it, killing defenseless prey. But studies of predators and their prey show that this isn't so. After observing tigers in Africa, Dr George Schaller wrote: 'The tiger's seemingly unbeatable array of weapons – its acute senses, great speed (but over short distances only), strength and size, and formidable claws and teeth – have given many naturalists the impression that the tiger can kill at will. . . . My experience shows quite the contrary – the tiger has to work quite hard for its meals. . . . I estimate that, for every wild prey killed, the tiger makes twenty to thirty unsuccessful attempts.'

Another biologist made the same observation about wolves. After studying North American wolves for twelve years, Dr L. David Mech concluded that these predators often fail to kill prey that they find. Also, wolves tend to kill animals that are either young, old, sick, weak,

32

injured or diseased. Dr Mech wrote: 'As is true with most predators, the wolf is an opportunist. . . . The predator takes whatever it can catch. If the wolf could capture prime, healthy prey, it certainly would. But most of the time it cannot. It happens that all the prey species of the wolf are well equipped with superb detection, defense, and escape systems. As long as these systems are in good working order, a prey animal is usually safe from wolf attack.'

Predators are usually bigger and fewer in number than the animals they prey upon. The reverse is true of *parasites*. These organisms live on or in other living things – their hosts, often spending an entire lifetime with them. In parasitism the parasite gets food and sometimes shelter, while the host gains nothing and may even suffer in some way from the relationship.

Very few living things are free of parasites, which are usually smaller and more numerous than their hosts. Indeed, many parasites have parasites of their own. Jonathan Swift exaggerated only a little when he wrote:

So, naturalists observe, a flea
Hath smaller fleas than on him prey;
And these have smaller still to bite 'em,
And so proceed *ad infinitum*.

Some biologists believe that most of the individual organisms now living are parasites, since there are many parasitic fungi, bacteria, flatworms, insects, ticks, and mites. Parasites are an important part of all communities, and like predators, often affect the number of other organisms in a community. Man has tried to use this ecological knowledge by deliberately bringing parasites or predators into an area where they might control the numbers of some pests. Sometimes this works well; often it does not.

In the 1870s, sugar-cane planters in Jamaica were losing about a fifth of their crops to rats, and a planter brought mongooses from India in hopes that they would prey on the rats. Within a few years the number of rats had dropped dramatically. The rats became harder to find. Then the mongooses began eating native mammals, ground-nesting birds, snakes, lizards, land crabs, and anything else they could find. They even took to eating sugar cane. Some of the creatures they wiped out had been useful controls on insect numbers, and the insect damage to sugar cane increased. The mongooses themselves became pests in need of control.

In another instance, house sparrows were brought to the United States from England in hopes that they would help control elm spanworms in New York City's Central Park. The birds did not control the insects and have spread across most of the nation, crowding out bluebirds and other native birds with which they compete for food and nesting sites.

People do learn from their mistakes, and experiences with mongooses, house sparrows, and other introduced organisms led to the passage of strict laws controlling the importation of plants and animals to the United States. The idea of using parasites and predators to control pests has not been abandoned; it is just done with much greater care and advance study. This method of limiting the number of pests is called

33

biological control, and there is hope that it will someday eliminate the need for many of the insect poisons used today.

The close association between parasite and host is an example of *symbiosis* which means 'living together'. There are a number of other examples of symbiosis in nature. In some relationships, one organism benefits and the other is not affected at all. This is called *commensalism*. Fish called remoras attach themselves to sharks. They get a free ride and eat fragments of the sharks' food. There are many other commensal relationships in the sea: Practically every worm burrow, shellfish, and sponge contains animals that depend on the host for shelter or food scraps. A biologist found 13,500 animals living within the pores of a large sponge collected off the Florida Keys. The animals were mostly small shrimps, but the total included nineteen species, among them a small fish.

In some symbiotic relationships, both organisms benefit. The most common and widespread example of this *mutualism* is a team of plants called lichen. You can find lichens clinging to rocks and tree trunks almost anywhere. Part of the lichen is a fungus. Within it are colonies of green algae cells. The fungus provides support and traps water which is used by the algae. The algae make food which is consumed by the fungus. Thus both kinds of plant benefit.

The organisms that make up a lichen couldn't survive long apart. In other cases of mutualism, the two organisms may be together only part of the time. Birds called egrets often perch on the backs of African mammals such as rhinoceroses. The birds feed on lice and ticks in the mammal's skin. This benefits both organisms. Also, the rhinoceros may be warned of danger when an egret flies in fright from its back. But neither species is so dependent on the other that it can't survive by itself.

(From *Ecology: Science of Survival* by Laurence Pringle)

Note your finishing time, reading time and reading speed. Check your reading speed against the table in the Appendix, p. 193.

The last two passages concentrate on *scanning* techniques.

Exercise 16

1 *Using the title/Anticipation.* Start by asking yourself some questions about the title 'Making artificial diamonds'. Perhaps you know something about artificial gems. Go over what you know. If you don't, have you any ideas at all about how it could be done?

2 Your *scanning* task is to check as quickly as possible whether the following statements are *true* or *false*.

　a) When the first artificial diamonds were finally
　　　made, the temperature used was 2900°F.　　　　　　true/false

　b) When the first artificial diamonds were made,
　　　the pressure used was 1,800,000 pounds to the
　　　square inch.　　　　　　　　　　　　　　　　　　true/false

c) The density of the artificial diamonds was 3·5
   grams per cubic centimetre.   true/false
d) Artificial diamonds and real diamonds are
   very similar but do not have the same atomic
   structure.   true/false
e) Artificial diamonds are just as beautiful as real
   diamonds.   true/false

3 Remember you are *scanning* not *reading fast* – so you do not
  have to read every word or even every paragraph.
4 When you have finished, go back to the beginning of the
  passage and *read* it in the usual way. Check your *reading speed*.
  Check the answers to your scanning task in the Appendix,
  p. 192.
5 Draw a diagram to represent the *organisation* of the passage.
6 Use the diagram to write a brief *summary* of the main points of
  the passage.

Note your starting time.

Making artificial diamonds

'It should be possible to make a precious stone that not only looks like
the real thing, but that *is* the real thing', said a chemist many years ago.
'The only difference should be that one crystal would be made by man,
the other by nature.'

At first this did not seem like a particularly hard task. Scientists began
to try making synthetic diamonds towards the end of the eighteenth
century. It was at this time that a key scientific fact was discovered:
diamonds are a form of carbon, which is a very common element.
Graphite, the black mineral that is used for the 'lead' in your pencil, is
made of it, too. The only difference, we know today, is that the carbon
atoms have been packed together in a slightly different way. The
chemists were fired with enthusiasm: Why not change a cheap and
plentiful substance, carbon, into a rare and expensive one, diamond?

You have probably heard about the alchemists who for centuries tried
to turn plain lead or iron into gold. They failed, because gold is
completely different from lead or iron. Transforming carbon into
diamonds, however, is not illogical at all. This change takes place in
nature, so it should be possible to make it happen in the laboratory.

It should be possible, but for one hundred and fifty years every effort
failed. During this period, none the less, several people believed that
they had solved the diamond riddle. One of these was a French scientist
who produced crystals that seemed to be the real thing. After the man's
death, however, a curious rumour began to go the rounds. The story
told that one of the scientist's assistants had simply put tiny pieces of
genuine diamonds into the carbon mixture. He was bored with the
work, and he wanted to make the old chemist happy.

The first real success came more than sixty years later in the
laboratories of the General Electric Company. Scientists there had been

working for a number of years on a process designed to duplicate nature's work. Far below the earth's surface, carbon is subjected to incredibly heavy pressure and extremely high temperature. Under these conditions the carbon turns into diamonds. For a long time the laboratory attempts failed, simply because no suitable machinery existed. What was needed was some sort of pressure chamber in which the carbon could be subjected to between 800,000 and 1,800,000 pounds of pressure to the square inch, at a temperature of between 2200° and 4400°F.

Building a pressure chamber that would not break under these conditions was a fantastically difficult feat, but eventually it was done. The scientists eagerly set to work again. Imagine their disappointment when, even with this equipment, they produced all sorts of crystals, but no diamonds. They wondered if the fault lay in the carbon they were using, and so they tried a number of different forms.

'Every time we opened the pressure chamber we found crystals. Some of them even had the smell of diamonds', recalls one of the men who worked on the project. 'But they were terribly small, and the tests we ran on them were unsatisfactory.'

The scientists went on working. The idea was then brought forward that perhaps the carbon needed to be dissolved in a melted metal. The metal might act as a catalyst, which means that it helps a chemical reaction to take place more easily.

This time the carbon was mixed with iron before being placed in the pressure chamber. The pressure was brought up to 1,300,000 pounds to the square inch and the temperature to 2900°F. At last the chamber was opened. A number of shiny crystals lay within. These crystals scratched glass, and even diamonds. Light waves passed through them in the same way as they do through diamonds. Carbon dioxide was given off when the crystals were burned. Their density was just 3·5 grams per cubic centimetre, as is true of diamonds. The crystals were analysed chemically. They were finally studied under X-rays, and there was no longer room for doubt. These jewels of the laboratory were not *like* diamonds; they *were* diamonds. They even had the same atomic structure. The atoms making up the molecule of the synthetic crystal were arranged in exactly the same pattern as they are in the natural.

'The jewels we have made are diamonds', says a physicist, 'but they are not very beautiful. Natural diamonds range in colour from white to black, with the white or blue-white favoured as gems. Most of ours are on the dark side, and are quite small.'

(From *The Artificial World Around Us* by Lucy Kavaler)

Note your finishing time, reading time and reading speed. Check your reading speed against the table in the Appendix, p. 193.

Exercise 17

1 *Using the title/Anticipation.* Ask yourself some questions about the title, 'Water clocks'.

2 Your *scanning* task is to check as quickly as possible whether the
   following statements are *true* or *false*.
   a) The passage says that clepsydras were used in
       America.   true/false
   b) Water clocks could not be used as striking
       clocks.   true/false
   c) Water clocks were used to time lawyers'
       speeches.   true/false
   d) Water clocks were superior to sundials in
       every way.   true/false
   e) Water clocks could not be used by travellers
       at sea.   true/false
3 When you have finished, go back to the beginning of the
   passage and *read* it in the usual way. Check your *reading speed*.
   Check your answers to the scanning task in the Appendix,
   p. 192.
4 Draw a diagram to represent the *organisation* of the passage.
5 Use the diagram to help you write a brief *summary* of the main
   points of the passage.

Note your starting time.

Water clocks

An early clock that could be used on cloudy days, at night, and indoors
was the clepsydra, or water clock. Although clepsydra is a Greek word
meaning *thief of water*, these clocks were probably first used in Egypt
about 2000 BC. They were also used for many years in Arabia, India,
China, Greece, Rome, and all of Europe.

The simplest clepsydra, like the sundial, needed just two parts – a
bowl with a small hole in the bottom, and a larger bowl marked off into
equal parts. Water was poured into the small bowl, and it dripped
slowly down into the large bowl. Usually it took an hour for the water
to rise from one line to the next in the large bowl.

Another simple type of water clock was used in India. It worked on
the principle opposite to the Egyptian clepsydra. A small empty bowl
with a hole in the bottom was set in a larger bowl full of water. Slowly
the small bowl filled with water and sank. As the water reached the lines
painted on the small bowl's sides, the time could be read.

Clepsydras could be much more complicated than this, however.
One model had a float with a notched rod rising from it. As the water
rose in the bowl, the float rose, and the notches in the rod fitted into the
cogs of a wheel that turned a pointer. The pointer marked the passing
hours on a round dial much like the clock faces of today.

An elegant water clock that could be heard as well as seen was made
in Persia over a thousand years ago as a gift to the Emperor
Charlemagne of France. The dial was made up of twelve doors, each
one representing an hour. Every hour a door opened, dropping the

proper number of metal balls on a brass gong. At twelve o'clock twelve tiny horsemen rode out and shut all the doors. This was probably one of the first striking clocks.

Clepsydras served an unusual purpose in the law courts of ancient Greece and Rome. Then, as now, speakers often talked too long. Before a trial the judge told each lawyer how long he could talk. The speeches were measured by the number of times the water ran through the clepsydra while the lawyer was talking. The clepsydras in courts usually held thirty gallons of water and required about twenty minutes to empty. Often lawyers tried to make the judge believe they needed more time than they had been given. Once in a while a lawyer even tried to cheat by putting small stones in the top part of the clepsydra so the water would run through more slowly.

Although the clepsydra had some advantages over the sundial, it had several disadvantages of its own. The water in the small bowl would not drip out at the same speed all the time unless the bowl was kept full. As the bowl began to empty, the water pressure decreased, and the water ran out more slowly. Also, the water always had to be clear, for muddy water runs more slowly.

In addition, the clepsydra could not be used in very cold countries. If the water froze, the clock stopped. Nor could it be used by a traveller. Anyone who has ever tried to hold a full cup of water in a moving car knows why a clepsydra could not be used on board a ship.

Perhaps the clepsydra's greatest disadvantage was its need for constant attention. Often there was a clepsydra in the town square. It was more practical to send a slave there to bring back the time than to keep water constantly running in a clepsydra at home.

(From *Clocks, from Shadow to Atom* by Kathryn Kilby Borland and Helen Ross Speicher)

Understanding graphic presentation

In academic writing, writers frequently present their data by means of diagrams, charts, etc. In this section we are going to look at some common methods of graphic presentation. You are also going to have a chance of producing some graphs and charts of your own – it is worth remembering in writing essays that the use of graphs and charts can do much to make your work more attractive, interesting and informative.

Exercise 18

Below is an example of the most straightforward way of presenting information, although not necessarily the easiest to interpret. The information is presented in the form of a *table* (tabular form). Use the data presented in the table to answer the questions that follow.

Table of leisure activities by social class in the U.K., 1970

Percentage

	Professional and managerial	Clerical	Skilled	Semi-skilled and unskilled	All
Proportion in each class doing selected activity at least monthly in previous year:					
Home-based activities					
Watching television	95	99	98	95	97
Gardening	70	62	66	50	64
Playing with children	59	63	66	59	62
Home decorations/repairs	52	55	56	45	53
Car cleaning	55	44	51	35	48
Playing an instrument	10	8	5	4	7
Total number of home-based activities engaged in at least monthly	*5·7*	*5·9*	*5·2*	*4·2*	*5·3*
Sporting activities					
Swimming	34	25	20	8	22
Fishing	9	3	9	5	8
Table tennis	10	10	4	2	6
Sailing	6	—	1	—	2
Total number of sporting activities engaged in at least monthly					
Active sports	*1·1*	*0·8*	*0·6*	*0·3*	*0·7*
Spectator sports	*0·4*	*0·3*	*0·5*	*0·3*	*0·4*
Other leisure activities					
Going for a drive	62	51	62	49	58
Going to a pub	51	42	54	58	52
Going for a walk	56	63	41	36	47
Going out for a meal	48	31	25	23	32
Attending church	22	20	12	7	15
Total number of activities engaged in at least monthly	*3·5*	*3·3*	*2·8*	*2·5*	*3·0*

(From *Facts in Focus* compiled by the Central Statistical Office)

1　What was the most popular activity among all social classes?
2　What was the most popular sporting activity?
3　What was the most popular leisure activity outside the home?
4　Comparing professional/managerial groups and skilled groups, which activities were
　　a)　more popular with the professional/managerial groups?
　　b)　more popular with the skilled group?
　　c)　the same for both groups?

5 Which activities were more popular with the clerical group than with any of the other groups?

6 What do you notice about the number of leisure activities taken by the semi-skilled and unskilled group as compared to the other groups?

7 (Discussion)   What do you think of the pattern of leisure activities of British people as shown here: are they using their leisure time in a sensible way?

8 (Discussion)   How do you think this table would compare with one drawn up for professional family men in your own country? Would the pattern of leisure be very different?

9 (Class research)   Find out the main leisure activities for the members of your class. List only activities which you are doing, or intend to do, on a regular basis. Express the results in a table.

Exercise 19

This example is a little bit more complicated since it is really two tables that can be compared.

Table of students' assessment of qualities of a good lecturer

Arts students

Proportion of students mentioning –	Cambridge	Leeds	Southampton
Delivery	57%	50%	36%
Notes	11%	8%	8%
Clarity	38%	45%	41%
Interest	49%	38%	41%
Originality	33%	32%	51%
Guidance	14%	30%	31%
Comprehensibility	6%	15%	21%
Grasp of subject	6%	13%	3%
Illustration	2%	5%	14%
Openness to questioning	1%	10%	13%
Factual coverage	1%	—	3%
Other	8%	2%	3%
Number of students	63	40	39

Science students

Proportion of students mentioning –	Cambridge	Leeds	Southampton	Northampton
Delivery	53%	37%	30%	22%
Notes	43%	37%	56%	20%
Clarity	59%	26%	32%	37%
Interest	37%	28%	23%	23%
Originality	2%	4%	2%	2%
Guidance	18%	24%	16%	22%
Comprehensibility	20%	26%	32%	45%
Grasp of subject	12%	13%	18%	42%
Illustration	6%	13%	14%	5%
Openness to questioning	—	13%	7%	5%
Factual coverage	4%	7%	5%	8%
Other	6%	4%	4%	8%
Number of students	49	46	57	92

(From *The Experience of Higher Education* by Peter Marris)

1 What were the three most important qualities of a good lecture according to the *Arts* students in
   a) Cambridge?
   b) Leeds?
   c) Southampton?
2 What were the three most important qualities of a good lecture according to the *Science* students in
   a) Cambridge?
   b) Leeds?
   c) Southampton?
   d) Northampton?
3 What differences do you notice between the stated preferences of the Arts and Science students?
4 Have you any suggestion why there should be these differences between Arts and Science students?
5 a) Look at the replies of the Arts students again. Do you notice any significant differences among the students' replies?
   b) Do the same for the replies of the Science students.
6 Have you any suggestion why there should be these differences from one university to another?
7 (Class research)
   a) Which qualities would you say were important for a good lecture? (1 for the most important, 2 for the next most important etc.)
   b) Compare notes with the other members of the class. Add up the totals. (The quality with the least number of points

will be the most important.) Compare your results with the three universities and one college listed.

(Note: In the original research, the students were not given ready-made categories, they were simply asked to write down what they took to be the qualities of a good lecture. Their replies were analysed and placed in categories by the researchers. All of the institutions researched are universities, except Northampton, which is a college of arts and technology.)

Exercise 20

Opposite is an example of one of the simplest kinds of chart, a bar chart. Use the information in the chart to answer the questions (all of which refer to 1973/74) which follow.

1 Roughly, what percentage of students were studying:
   a) Science?
   b) Medicine etc?
   c) Education?
2 In which subject areas were women students well represented (i.e. at least 20% of total)?
3 In which subject areas were the number of women students about the same as, or more than, the number of men students?
4 What were the three most popular subjects areas?
5 Does the number of students in the various subject areas surprise you (i.e. would you have expected any subject area to be more, or less, popular)?
6 (Discussion) Can you suggest why certain subjects seem to be much more popular with women than others? Would it be the same in all countries, do you think?

Bar chart of subject group of study for university full-time students in the U.K., 1973/74

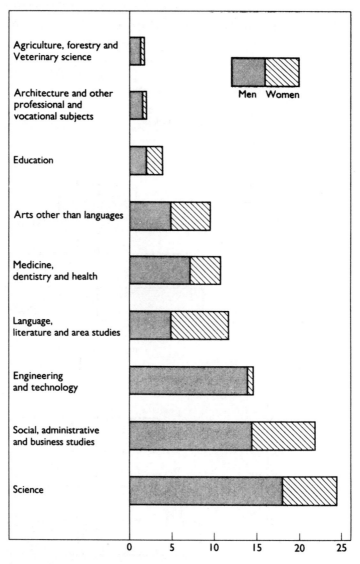

(From *Facts in Focus* compiled by the Central Statistical Office)

Exercise 21

Here is a slightly more complicated form of bar chart.

Bar chart of population and age distribution of the U.K., 1901/1974

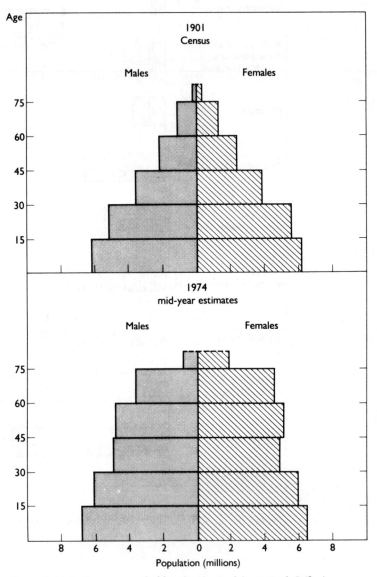

(From *Facts in Focus* compiled by the Central Statistical Office)

1 How does the total number of people living in Britain in 1974 compare with 1901?
2 In what age-groups has the biggest increase in population taken place?
3 In the 1974 estimates, how does the number of men and women compare
   a) under 15 years?
   b) over 75 years?
4 Roughly, quantify your answers to 3 above (i.e. give approximate numbers of men and women).
   a) under 15 years
   b) over 75 years
5 a) What do you notice about the 'shapes' of the two charts for 1901 and 1974?
   b) Can you suggest some reasons for the differences in the shapes?
6 (Discussion)   Do you think the 1901 shape is a better one for the country than the 1974 shape?

Exercise 22

The example below is a combination of two different kinds of graph: a *line graph* ('Vehicles with licences current') and a *surface graph* ('Casualties'). You will see why they have been given these names.

Combined line graph of vehicles with licences current and surface graph of road casualties

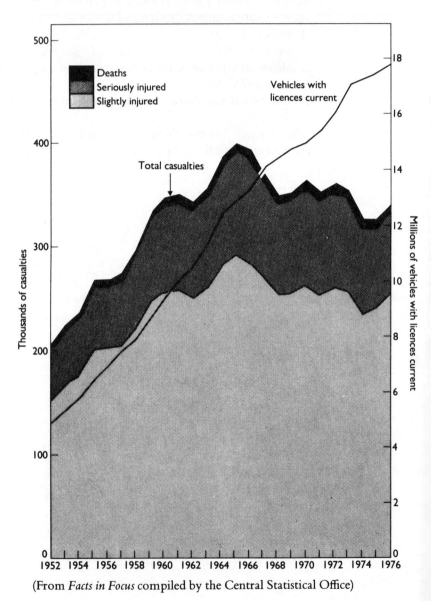

(From *Facts in Focus* compiled by the Central Statistical Office)

(All answers involving numbers can be very approximate.)

1 How many vehicles had current road licences in
   a) 1950?
   b) 1962?
   c) 1974?
2 How many road casualties were there in
   a) 1950?
   b) 1962?
   c) 1974?
3 What was the worst year for road accidents in Britain?
4 How many casualties were there that year?
5 Does the *proportion* of people killed, seriously injured and slightly injured remain roughly the same from year to year, or not?
6 What is there that might be thought unexpected or puzzling about this graph?
7 Have you any explanation for this rather unexpected fact?

Exercise 23

Here are two examples of what is called, for obvious reasons, a *pie-graph* or a *circle-graph*.

Pie-graph (circle-graph) of household expenditure in the U.K., 1973

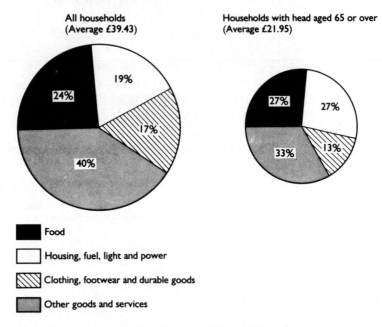

All households
(Average £39.43)

Households with head aged 65 or over
(Average £21.95)

■ Food

□ Housing, fuel, light and power

▨ Clothing, footwear and durable goods

▨ Other goods and services

(From Central Statistical Office, *Social Trends* No. 6.)

1 Why is the right-hand pie-graph smaller than the left-hand one?
2 When compared to the 'over 65' household
  a) what things does the average household spend more on?
  b) what things does the average household spend less on?
3 On both budgets
  a) what is the most important item?
  b) what is the least important item?
4 Very roughly,
  a) what did the average household spend on food in 1973?
  b) what did the average 'over 65' household spend on 'other goods and services'?
5 (Discussion)   Could you try to account for the differences between the two groups?
6 (Class research)   If you made up a pie-graph for your own expenditure, what would the main sections be? What would the graph look like? Draw it roughly, and compare yours with someone else's.

Exercise 24

The kind of chart illustrated below is called a *histogram*.
Histograms are very often used to show how frequently
something occurs, or how common something is over a given
range – in this case, a period of time.

Histogram of students' private study time

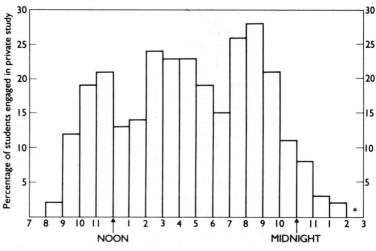

* One per cent of students were recorded as studying between 2.00 and 2.15 a.m.

(From Central Statistical Office, *Social Trends* No. 5 (simplified))

Assuming the data given in the histogram to be true for a given
group of students, answer these questions:

1 What is the most popular time for private study among the
   students?
2 What proportion of the student body is studying at that time?
3 What is the most popular time for private study
   a) in the afternoon?   b) in the morning?
4 What proportions of the student population study
   a) before 9 a.m.?   b) after midnight?
5 What are the periods when more than 20% of the student
   population are doing private study?
6 The chart is not even, but goes up and down. Can you explain
   these 'mountains and valleys'?
7 Do you think that the most 'popular' periods are necessarily a
   matter of the students' personal choice?
8 (Discussion and class research)   When do you usually do your
   private study? Compare notes with the rest of the class and
   make a histogram.

49

Exercise 25

Below is an example of a special kind of chart used for describing complicated processes. It is called an *algorithm*. It shows you how to make a local telephone call in Britain (not usually a very complicated process!).

Algorithm for making a local telephone call

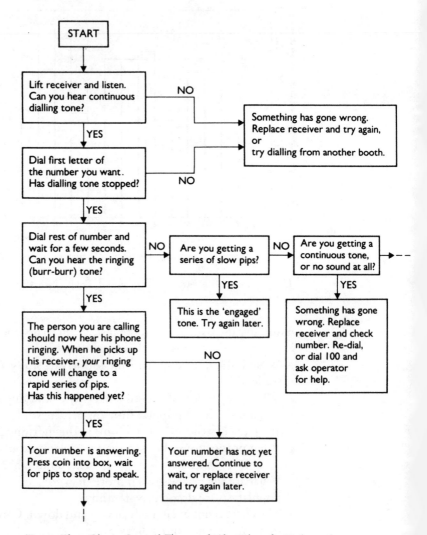

(From *Flow Charts, Logical Trees and Algorithms for Rules and Regulations* by B. N. Lewis, I. S. Horbin and C. P. Gane)

1 a) What advantages do you think algorithms have over the ordinary way of printing advice or instructions?

b) Do algorithms have any disadvantages compared to the normal presentation?

c) In what sort of situation do you think an algorithm would be more helpful than the normal method of presentation?

2 Below is a set of instructions for *finding a particular book in the library*. See if you can present the same information in the form of an algorithm.

Finding a particular book in the library

Let us imagine that someone has mentioned to you a book called *Recent Developments in Thermodynamics* which he has recently returned to the College/University library, and you have decided that you wish to borrow it.

Finding a particular book in the library is quite easy if you know both the author's name and the title of the book. You simply go to the *author catalogue*, which is alphabetically arranged. You will find a card with the author's name, the title of the work and the shelf-mark, which tells whereabouts in the library the book is kept. You will go to the appropriate shelf, take the book and get it stamped at the issue desk.

If the book is not there, it means that someone has got it out. In that case, you can go to the issue desk and reserve it.

If you do not know the author, but only the title, see if the library has a *title catalogue*. If it has check it up in the same way as you did with the author catalogue. If there is no title catalogue, then it should have a *subject catalogue*. You will have to check through all the titles under that subject until you find the one you are looking for. The card with the title on it will also have a shelf-mark, and then you proceed as we mentioned before.

(Note: a more complete account of these procedures is to be found in unit 5.)

Unit 3 Taking notes

The aims of note taking

Almost everyone who studies has to take notes at some time.
But have you ever asked yourself the reason for taking notes?
There are usually three main reasons:
1 to have a record of the speaker's or writer's main ideas.
   (Notice: *not* to take down or copy every word.)
2 to help one's memory when revising, e.g. before an
   examination.
3 to make what the speaker or writer says a part of your own
   knowledge.

This section will teach you how to achieve these aims by *positive*
note taking. You are a student *not* a tape-recorder or a secretary
who knows shorthand! For the same reason, if you are taking
notes from a book or article it is generally not a good idea to copy
out large chunks of the text, unless you are going to quote it
verbatim, i.e. word for word.

Exercise 1

Read through the following list of methods of recording
information:
notes taken while listening
notes taken while reading
notes taken from memory
shorthand notes
tape recording
photocopying
underlining etc.

Discuss the advantages and disadvantages of the methods listed
with your tutor. Which methods are you able to use at the
moment? Which methods do you think would be most useful to
you? Remember to ask yourself *why* you need to take notes.

Exercise 2

What do you mean by a *good* lecture? (If you have done exercise
19 in unit 2, you will have some ideas about this.) Are lectures

out-of-date? Will books (and perhaps television) ever make
lectures unnecessary? Discuss with your tutor.

Exercise 3

When you have finished your discussion, make a list of the main
advantages and disadvantages of a) learning from lectures, b)
learning from books.

Taking notes from a text

The first thing to do is to *survey* the text (see unit 2 for more
information on this). The purpose of the survey is to acquaint
yourself with the text, so that you can quickly find out what the
writer's main points are, what he is driving at. Surveying is
something you cannot do with a lecture, so take advantage of it.
But remember that it should be done quickly.

Then read the text again quickly *making a note of the main points*
and how they relate to one another. This can be done mentally (if
the text is a short, uncomplicated one); or on the text itself by
underlining (if the text is your own!); or directly into your
notebook.

If you are writing the main points in a notebook, put them
down in some way that relates them to one another. If you can
put the information in the form of a *diagram*, do so. Diagrams are
usually easier to remember. If you decide to use *a list* (which is
often the most convenient method) there are various listing,
systems one can use – the table below gives some examples.
Choose a system and stick to it. It could be very confusing to
switch from one system to another.

Listing and numbering

Arabic numerals	1, 2, 3, 4, 5, etc.
Decimal system	1.1, 1.2, 1.3, 2.1, 2.2, etc. (Not usually combined with other systems. Subdivisions are usually also decimalised e.g. 2.1.1, 2.1.2 etc)
Large roman numerals	I, II, III, IV, V, VI, VII, VIII, IX, X, etc.
Small roman numerals (usually in brackets)	(i), (ii), (iii), (iv), (v), (vi), (vii), (viii), (ix), (x), etc.
Capital letters	A, B, C, D, E, etc.

Small letters (often in brackets)	(a), (b), (c), (d), (e), etc.

Except for the decimal system, these systems can be used in combination. Compare:

I		1	
II	A	2	(a)
	B		(b)
	1		(i)
	2		(ii)
	3		(iii)
	4		(iv)
III	A	3	(a)
	B		(b)
	C		(c)
IV		4	

Exercise 4

Below are some headings from a lecture on 'Communication'. There are three main sections to the talk: Non-electronic methods (i.e. methods which do not use electricity), Electronic methods, and the Use of satellites. Use *numbering* to show how the topics fit into one another. The notes will also be clearer if you use *spacing*, i.e. start some lines further in from the margin than others to make your message clear. Use a large sheet (A4-size if you have it). Use the full length of the page.

Communication

NON-ELECTRONIC METHODS
messengers
human messengers
birds as messengers – pigeons
signals
signals that can be seen
smoke signals
lighthouses
semaphore
handwriting
printed books
newspapers
signals that can be heard
drums
horns (motor-horns, fog-horns)

ELECTRONIC METHODS
using wires
telephones
cables
without using wires
radio
television
radio-telephone
cinema

THE USE OF SATELLITES
communication satellites
weather satellites
navigation satellites

Exercise 5

Read the information that is given here about musical
instruments. Then arrange it in note form, and try to show by
numbering, spacing etc how the different items of information
relate to one another.

Musical instruments

There are many different kinds of musical instruments. They are divided
into three main classes according to the way that they are played. For
example, some instruments are played by blowing air into them. These
are called *wind* instruments. In some of these the air is made to vibrate
inside a wooden tube, and these are said to be of the *woodwind* family.
Examples of woodwind instruments are the flute, the clarinet and the
bassoon. Other instruments are made of *brass*: the trumpet and the horn,
for example. There are also various other wind instruments such as the
mouth-organ and the bagpipes.

Some instruments are played by banging or striking them. One
obvious example is the drum, of which there are various kinds.
Instruments like this are called *percussion* instruments.

The last big group of musical instruments are the ones which have
strings. There are two main kinds of *stringed* instrument: those in which
the music is made by plucking the strings, and those where the player
draws a bow across the strings. Examples of the former are the harp and
the guitar. Examples of the latter are the violin and the cello.

Look at the passage below. Arrange it in note form, using headings, numbering etc.

Acquiring information

What are the ways in which a student can acquire information? Firstly, he will acquire information from his tutors, in three main ways – by lecture, by tutorial and by handouts which the tutor may give him. Secondly, he may acquire information from 'other experts' outside his college: principally by reading but also perhaps by listening to the radio, listening to cassette recordings, or watching educational TV programmes. Thirdly, he will get information from his fellow students: perhaps in student-led seminars, perhaps in the contributions of other students in tutorial, or perhaps just in informal conversation. Lastly, he can acquire information from himself! By thinking about his subject and linking together what he has heard and seen, he may come up with new ideas, which are his alone.

Exercise 7

Here is an article giving advice on considerations to bear in mind when buying a calculator. Summarise the advice in note form. Use headings, numbering etc. Do not attempt to record the first and last paragraphs.

Buying a pocket calculator

In recent years, pocket calculators have become almost as commonplace as wristwatches. There is now a tremendous choice of calculators at a great variety of prices.

The following points should be borne in mind when buying a calculator. Firstly, there is the number of things the calculator can do. The most basic type of calculators have simply the four arithmetical functions (addition, subtraction, multiplication and division), with perhaps a few other functions like percentage and square root. Next, there are calculators with a 'memory' which allows you to store information, do more calculations and recall the information when you need it. There are also *special purpose* calculators for, say, scientific, mathematical, statistical or other uses, with the appropriate functions. Some more expensive calculators are *programmable*, i.e. there is a choice of complex calculating routines which will be done automatically. Lastly, some calculators can *print out* the calculations, so that you can check the calculations as they are being done, and also have a permanent record of them.

The second important question is how easy the calculator is to use. The display of figures should be *clear* so that the figures are easily distinguished – also, watch out for the decimal point! In some calculators it is not very easy to see. The display should also be *bright*, so that it can be read in any light. Next, the keys. They should be the *right size and shape* to be easily pressed – some calculators look very neat but are awkward to use. For the same reason, there should be a reasonable space between the keys. It is also more convenient if each key has only one function: two-function keys can be tricky to use. Some people also like it if the keys *click* (give a sound) when the calculator has been registered.

The third important point is the *power unit*. Calculators may be *mains-operated* (i.e. run by electricity from a wall-plug) or *battery-operated*. Mains-operated calculators are cheaper to run if you use them a lot, but not so convenient for occasional use (or in an exam room!). Battery-operated calculators may be run by ordinary batteries, or by special 'long-life' batteries, or by rechargeable batteries. It may also be possible to buy a *mains adaptor*, which will allow you to run a battery calculator off the mains, when that is convenient.

(If a calculator is important to your studies, there will probably be other features to be taken into consideration. Consult with your tutor before you make your final choice.)

Semantic markers

When you are listening to a lecture or reading a text, watch out for the use of semantic markers. These are words or phrases which serve as signals for the meaning and structure of the lecture or text. They tell us how the ideas are organised.

Functions of semantic markers

1 The markers may be used for listing, such as:

firstly	thirdly
in the first place	my next point is
secondly	last/finally

2 They may show us the cause and effect relationship between one idea and another:

so	because
therefore	since
thus (we see)	

3 They can indicate that the speaker or writer is going to illustrate his ideas by giving examples:

| for instance | let's take . . . |
| for example | an example/instance of this was . . . |

4 They may introduce an idea which runs against what has been said, or is going to be said:

but	and yet
nevertheless	although
on the other hand	

5 A very important kind of semantic marker is one which shows

that the speaker or writer is about to sum up his message, or
part of it:

to summarise	it amounts to this
in other words	if I can just sum up
what I have been saying is this	

6 Semantic markers may be used to express a time relationship:

then	previously
next	while
after that	when

7 They may be used to indicate the relative importance of
something. The following are markers of *emphasis*:
it is worth noting
I would like to direct your attention to
(For more examples of markers in this category, see
pp. 62–3.)
8 They may be used to re-phrase what has already been said, or
to introduce a definition:

in other words	to put it another way
let me put it this way	that is to say

9 Also, to express a condition:

if	assuming that
unless	

These are only a few examples of semantic markers. Train
yourself to listen for these key words and phrases.

Exercise 8

Look at passage A. Read it through, noting down or underlining
all the semantic markers.

Passage A

Since World War II, DDT and other organic insecticides have been used
in large quantities. Tens of thousands of tons are produced each year.
The United States alone spent over a billion dollars for such insecticides
in the single year of 1966.

Not only are our crops saved but the various insect-spread diseases are
all but wiped out. Since DDT wipes out mosquitoes and flies, as well as
lice, malaria is now almost unknown in the United States. Less than a
hundred cases a year are reported and almost all are brought in from
abroad.

Yet this does not represent a happy ending. The use of organic
insecticides has brought troubles in its train. Sometimes such insecticides
don't work because they upset the balance of nature.

For instance, DDT might be fairly deadly to an insect we want to kill,
but even more deadly to another insect that lives on the first one. Only a
few harmful insects survive but their insect enemies are now all dead. In

a short time, the insects we don't want are more numerous than they were before the use of DDT.

Then, too, organic insecticides don't kill all species of insects. Some insects have a chemical machinery that isn't affected by these poisons; they are 'resistant'. It may happen that a resistant insect could do damage to our crops but usually doesn't because some other insect is more numerous and gets the lion's share of the food.

If DDT kills the damaging insect, but leaves the resistant insect behind, then that resistant insect can multiply enormously. It then becomes a great danger and DDT can't touch it.

In fact, even among those species of insects that are killed by DDT there are always a few individuals that differ chemically from the rest and are resistant. They survive when all other individuals are killed. They multiply and then a whole species of resistant insects comes into existence.

Thus, as the years pass, DDT has become less effective on the house fly, for instance. Some resistance was reported as early as 1947, and this has been growing more serious. By now almost every species of insect has developed resistance, including the body louse that spreads typhus.

Finally, even though organic insecticides are not very poisonous to creatures other than insects, they are not entirely harmless either. If too much insecticide is used, some birds can be poisoned. Fish are particularly easy to kill, and if insecticides are used on water to kill young insects, young fish may also go in great numbers.

(From *Twentieth Century Discovery* by Isaac Asimov)

Exercise 9

Do the same for passage B.

Passage B

The need for money originates from the fact that different people in society produce different things. This means that people depend on each other for goods and services. Let us take the case of a farmer who produces more food than he requires and a carpenter who lives by selling the tables and chairs that he has made. It will be obvious that unless some means of exchange is found, the farmer will not be able to get rid of his surplus food and the carpenter will starve! Clearly, the simplest means of exchange will be for them to use barter – in other words, to exchange a certain amount of one kind of goods (let's say flour) for a certain amount of another (tables or chairs, in this case).

Obviously, barter can work only in a very simple society. In an advanced society one cannot go around carrying things in the hope that we can exchange them for the things we need.

So we need something which will stand for the goods and services that we want to exchange. Hence the origin of money. It follows that anything can act as money or currency, provided that all the people using it agree on its value. We are not surprised to find, therefore, the use of very many different kinds of money at one time or another.

Examples of 'currencies' that have been used in the past are cowrie shells, coconuts, whales' teeth and salt. As one might expect, things used as money have certain qualities, namely that they should be firstly convenient, secondly durable (that is, long lasting) and lastly of some rarity value. Thus we would *not* expect large stones to be used as money (because they are too inconvenient), fruit or plants (because they go bad eventually), nor pebbles (because they are too common). Nevertheless, it is interesting to note that these rules do not work all the time. To take one good example, there is an island in the Pacific Ocean where the natives used large stone wheels as currency; sometimes these wheels were as big as twelve feet across! They were sometimes stored outside a man's house as a sign of his wealth.

Exercise 10

Now go over both passages again, and take a look at the semantic markers you have noted. Decide which of the nine functions listed above each marker is fulfilling. Put the figure 1, 2, 3, etc beside each marker, according to its function. If you think that you have found a marker, the function of which has not been listed, make a note of it, and indicate its function.

Taking notes from a lecture i) Before the lecture

Positive note taking starts *before* a lecture!

Imagine that you are sitting in a lecture-hall about to hear a lecture. If you have already received some lectures on the same subject, glance through your notes on the last one quickly to refresh your memory.

If you know the topic or title of the lecture in advance, try asking yourself some questions about it: Do you know anything about the topic at all? What do you expect to learn? How will it relate to other topics that have been discussed? How do you think it will relate to your job/your own interests/your own opinions on this subject? Questions like these will give you a *positive* attitude even before you put pen to paper. They will therefore make it easier to integrate the new information, i.e. to make it a part of your active knowledge.

Exercise 11

Here are some possible headings for lectures. Choose two or more of the headings, and put down *three* questions which you would expect the lecture to answer.
1 *Man's place in the universe*   (Lecture by an astronomer)
2 *Problems of weather prediction*   (Lecture by a meteorologist, i.e. weather expert)

3 *If you are ill, it's probably your own fault!* (Popular talk by a doctor)
4 *Sharing the ocean's wealth* (Talk by an economist)
5 *Influences on human development* (Lecture by a psychologist)
6 *Children and books* (Talk by a librarian)
7 *The family in the twentieth century* (Lecture by a sociologist)
8 *Teenagers and drug-addiction* (Lecture by a sociologist)

Basic equipment
Very simply: pens and notepaper. Obviously there is some degree of personal choice here. You should choose what suits yourself. Nevertheless, there are some points worth bearing in mind.
1 *Pens.* Whatever you find pleasant to use. It may be an idea to have more than one colour of pen at your disposal. You can also get ball point pens which contain two or more colours. Colour contrasts can do a lot to make information stand out.
2 *Notebooks.* It is best to choose a *standard size of notebook*. A4 is a good size because it gives you room to lay out your notes properly. Smaller notebooks are handy for carrying around but your notes can get cramped. It is also better to have the pages *ready-punched* so that they can fit into the appropriate loose-leaf binder.

Having your notes in a loose-leaf binder means you can later re-arrange them to suit your convenience: for example, you can take pages out if you need them, or you can put *in*, say, photocopies of relevant articles, newspaper clippings etc at the appropriate place to relate to your notes.

If you sometimes have to take notes in, say, a seminar room where there is nothing convenient to lean on, then *a clipboard* may be useful. (For examples of these and other useful materials for recording and storing information see the Appendix, p. 194.)

Exercise 12

Look at the materials in the Appendix, p. 194. Make a list of those which appear to you: a) necessary; b) desirable.
Now check the prices at a bookshop or stationers. (You may find that what is desirable is also very expensive.)

Exercise 13

Listen to the short talk on 'Volcanoes' on tape. During the talk, take notes in the way that you would normally do.

Exercise 14

1 What sort of notebook did you use? Is it entirely satisfactory for your needs?
2 Were your notes cramped together or well spread out? Which is better?
3 Did you think of using a diagram? Look at the model notes in the Appendix, p. 196. Do you think the diagram in the model notes makes things clearer?
4 Did you use shading or colour in your notes? Notice the use of shading in the model notes.
5 Did you use PRINTING and _underlining_?
6 Was your information systematically arranged?

Taking notes from a lecture ii) The main ideas

Unless, for some reason, you wish to record every word that the lecturer says, you will have to select what you want to write down. You will naturally want to select the main points, and perhaps some subordinate or subsidiary points which relate to the main points. How does one recognise the main points?

Usually, the speaker will make it clear which ideas he wishes to emphasise by the way in which he presents them. In other words, the main ideas are cued. They are often cued by such semantic markers as:

I would like to emphasise . . .
The general point you must remember is . . .
It is important to note that . . .
I repeat that . . .
The next point is crucial to my argument . . .

Very often speakers _list_ their main points (see the section on semantic markers, p. 58).

Other ways in which lecturers may cue their main points while speaking are by _emphasis_ or _repetition_; or perhaps by _visual display_ (e.g. by putting headings on a blackboard, overhead projector etc).

Sometimes you will find that the _facial expression_ and _gestures_ of the lecturer point up his meaning (of course, you will not see these if you are crouched over your notes, scribbling away furiously!).

Often _examples_ and _points of lesser importance_ are also cued. The speaker may use such phrases as:

Let me give you some examples . . .
For instance . . .
I might add . . .
To illustrate this point . . .

Examples and points of lesser importance should be related
briefly to the main headings.

Sometimes speakers will *digress*, i.e. mention things which have
very little to do with their main topic, or relate to it only in a
rather roundabout way. Speakers will sometimes digress
deliberately in order to give more spice or variety to their
lectures, or because the digression is interesting, amusing or
topical. There is, of course, no need to note down digressions.
Digression markers are expressions like:

By the way . . .
I might note in passing . . .

Exercise 15

You will hear some extracts from eight different lectures. For
each extract write down whether you think it is a *main point*,
example, or *digression*. The purpose of the exercise is to train you
in spotting these different parts of a lecture. Discuss with your
tutor why you think the extract falls under the heading you have
chosen.

Exercise 16

The purpose of this exercise and the following one is to give you
practice in sorting out main ideas from subordinate (i.e. less
important, supporting) ideas. You are going to hear a short
lecture on the position of trade unions in Britain in the early
1970s. Take a blank A4-size sheet of paper, and draw a line down
the middle of it, dividing it into two sections. On the left-hand
side put the heading *Main ideas*, and on the right-hand side, the
heading *Subordinate ideas*. Listen to the lecture and take brief notes
(headings), putting each note or heading in the appropriate
section. You will probably find that you will end up with three
main ideas, and six (or so) subordinate ideas.

Exercise 17

Do this in the same way as the previous exercise. The lecture is a
continuation of the previous topic. Again, you will probably
have three main ideas, and eight (or so) subordinate ideas.

Using abbreviations

We have said that the student is not concerned with taking down every word that the lecturer says, so have rejected shorthand for normal note taking. Nevertheless, a lot of time and effort can be saved by using abbreviations and symbols. The main point to remember is to use only abbreviations which you will be able to remember when revising your notes some time later. A student of linguistics, for example, might be ill-advised to use *phon.* as an abbreviation for *phonology*: it could equally well stand for *phonetics*, a related, but different, area of linguistics.

Abbreviations can be of three kinds:

1 *Field abbreviations.* The student specialising in a certain field will learn certain abbreviations as part of the study of that field. For example, a student of chemistry will know that C stands for Carbon, and Ca for Calcium. Such abbreviations are very useful since they are widely used within each field but not ambiguous, or liable to be misunderstood.

2 *Commonly understood abbreviations.* These are abbreviations in common use, or else easily understood. Some examples are *i.e.* meaning *that is*, and = meaning *is equal to*, or *is the same as*. For more examples see table below.

Some useful abbreviations and symbols for note taking

From Latin		Symbols			
cf.	compare (with)	∴	therefore, thus, so	≫	much greater than
e.g.	for example	∵	because	≪	much less than
etc.	et cetera, and so on	=	is equal to, the same as	≧	equal to, or greater than
et al.	and others				
ibid.	in the same place (in a book or article)	≠	is not equal to, not the same as	%	per cent
i.e.	that is	+	plus, and, more	÷	divide, divided by
N.B.	note well (something important)	−	minus, less	×	multiply, multiplied by
		>	greater than	⌐	insert (something which has been omitted)
viz.	namely (naming someone or something you have just referred to)	<	less than		
		∝	proportional to	→	from . . . . to, leads to, results in
		∝̸	not proportional to		

3 *Personal abbreviations made up by the student himself.* If you find yourself having to frequently note down a certain word it is sensible to find a way of abbreviating it. For example, a student of English literature listening to a lecture on the poet Wordsworth could well use the initial W. instead of writing out the poet's name in full each time he has to refer to it.

Exercise 18

Take a sheet of A4 paper (or whatever size you normally use for your notebook). On it make a note of any symbols from the table above which you are not very familiar with but which you think may be useful to you. Note down also on the same sheet any other abbreviations which you frequently use or find useful.

Exercise 19

Here are some notes taken by a student from an encyclopedia article on pyramids. Since these are supposed to be rough notes for his own use, you can see that the student has wasted quite a lot of time by writing out everything in full. See if you can write his notes more briefly by using abbreviations and leaving out unnecessary words.

Pyramids

By the word 'pyramid' we usually mean the grave of an Egyptain king of the Old and Middle Kingdoms (that is, from 2680 BC to 1567 BC).

The earliest pyramid was built for King Zoser and is called the 'Step Pyramid' because the sides go up in large steps. It is 197 feet high.

The largest pyramid ever made is one of a group of three built at Giza, south of Cairo, by the kings of the fourth dynasty, which lasted from 2680 BC to 2565 BC. This pyramid is called the 'Great Pyramid', and was built by King Khufu (his Greek name is Cheops). The outside of this pyramid consists of more than two million blocks of stone. The average weight of each of these blocks is two and a half tons.

Exercise 20

Here is another exercise on the same lines as the previous one.

Malta

Malta is comprised of three islands. They are the islands of Malta itself, and the smaller islands of Gozo and Comino. The area of Malta island is ninety-five square miles, while Gozo is twenty-six square

miles in area; the size of Comino is only one square
mile. The total area is therefore a bit smaller
than the Isle of Wight in the United Kingdom.

As at 1970 the population was 322,173. The
capital city is Valetta. Valetta has a magnificent
harbour. The Maltese have their own language which
is mainly derived from Arabic but also contains many
Sicilian words.

The chief products are potatoes, vegetables,
grapes, wheat and barley. Malta is a very important
shipping centre for the Mediterranean and is of great
strategic value.

(As a check on your use of abbreviations, you might try
writing your answers to exercises 19 and 20 out in full without
looking at this text; or read them aloud to another student who
has the text in front of him.)

Branching notes

This is a type of note taking which is especially useful when you
have not been given an outline of the lecture. It enables you to
develop your notes as the lecture proceeds, in a flexible way. It is
also argued that this type of layout makes it easier to recapture the
speaker's original message and to see the relationships between
ideas more clearly.

Here is a procedure which you might try to follow:
1 Have, if possible, a double-page spread of notepaper in front of
   you. You may find it better to have the pages spread
   breadthwise: i.e. with the broad part going from left to right.
2 Take notes only on one of the double pages. The blank facing
   pages can always be used for adding more information, or for
   'reconstituting' notes, i.e. re-writing your notes in a fuller or
   more convenient form.
3 For any kind of note taking, always make a habit of noting the
   lecturer's name, the subject and date of the lecture. (Noting the
   lecturer's name can be useful if for any reason you wish to
   contact him outside the lecture room. Dating lectures helps to
   keep them in the correct sequence.)
4 Put the topic of the lecture *in the centre of the page*. (If it is not
   made clear what the central topic of the lecture is, then put the
   first topic there.)

5 Relate all the other topics to it, and to one another, by lines. This technique can be best explained by an example. Check back to exercise 6, the short article entitled 'Acquiring information'. Here is the information in list form:

Aquiring information

1 from tutors
  a) lecture
  b) tutorial
  c) handout

2 'other experts'
  a) reading
  b) radio
  c) cassettes
  d) TV

3 fellow students
  a) seminars
  b) tutorials
  c) conversation

4 student himself – can develop new ideas.

Now look at the notes on page 68. You will see the same in *branching* form. There are no golden rules about the 'correct' form of the branching. Two students may put the information down in different ways and still have good notes. PRINT your headings (i.e. write them in capital letters) if at all possible – it will make it easier to follow your notes when you are revising. Make your headings as concise as possible (this applies to list notes too, of course).

Exercise 21

Here are some outline notes on the article 'Buying a pocket calculator', exercise 7.

Buying a pocket calculator

1 things it can do
  a) arithmetical functions
  b) memory
  c) special purpose
  d) programmable
  e) print out

Branching notes (Example)

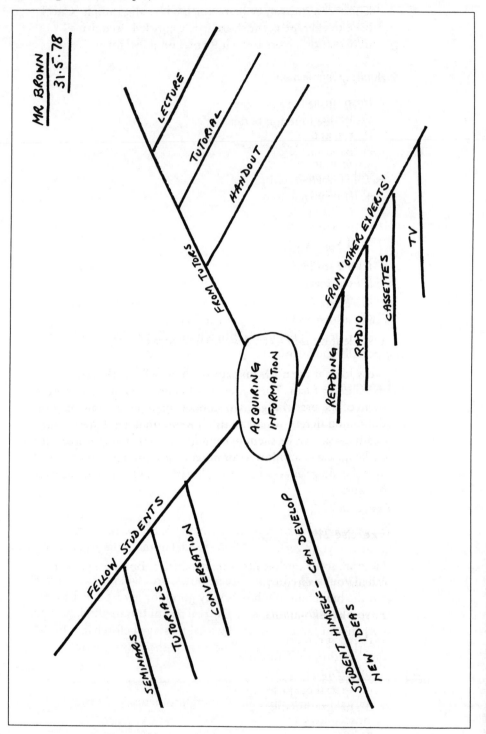

2 ease of use
  a) display
      i) clear
      ii) bright
  b) keys
      i)   size
      ii) shape
      iii) space between keys
      iv) one function better
      v)   click

3 power unit
  a) mains–operated
  b) battery–operated
      i)   ordinary b.
      ii) long–life b.
      iii) rechargeable b.
  c) mains adaptor
(Notice the use of abbreviations to save time)

Take a blank sheet of paper and put down how you think this should appear in branching form. When you have done this compare it with the model notes in the Appendix, p. 201. Note especially the use of arrows to link related points.

Exercise 22

To give yourself some practice in doing branching notes and seeing how they compare with list notes, look back at the notes you made for exercise 16 (p. 63) and re-write them in the form of branching notes. Compare your version with the model notes in the Appendix, p. 202.

Exercise 23

Do the same for the notes that you made for exercise 17. Compare your version with the model notes in the Appendix, p. 203.

When you have compared these notes, you will probably agree that the branching method is very good for giving a picture of the speaker's total message. The real test of this method, however, is when you cannot survey the total message beforehand. In the next three exercises you will hear some short lectures on tape.

Exercise 24

a) Listen to the lecture on 'Solving problems' and make branching notes.

b) When you have finished, expand your notes into connected writing, and compare your expanded notes with the transcript in the Appendix, p. 204. Don't worry if your notes are slightly different from someone else's. Note taking is to some extent a personal thing.

Exercise 25

a) Listen to the lecture on 'Communication' and make branching notes.
b) As in the previous exercise, expand your notes and compare with the transcript in the Appendix, p. 207.

Exercise 26

a) Listen to the lecture on 'How to present a seminar paper'.
b) Expand your notes and compare with the transcript in the Appendix, p. 209.

The parts of a lecture

You may have noticed by now that many lectures can be divided into three parts:

1 *Introduction*. The lecturer 'sets the scene' for his lecture. He may revise what he said last time. He will probably give you some outline idea of what he is going to say this time.
2 *Main part of the lecture*. Here he will make his points, with examples.
3 *End summary*. The speaker may round off his lecture by going over the main points again, or by briefly stating his point of view.

Exercise 27

See if you can spot the different parts of the lectures you have heard so far. Look at the texts of the lectures on 'British trade unions' in the Appendix, pp. 198 and 199.

Taking each of the two lectures in turn, see if you can identify the introduction, main part, and end summary.

Exercise 28

Do the same for the lectures on 'Communication' (Appendix, p. 207) and 'How to present a seminar paper' (Appendix, p. 209). Discuss your findings with your tutor.

Note taking and reconstituting: practice

Exercises 29 and 30·

a) For the last two lectures on 'Marriage customs' and 'Computers' make notes as you listen. They could be either branching or list notes. When you have finished the notes for both lectures try and answer the questions below, using your notes. Remember: do not look at the questions, until you have finished your notes.

b) Expand your notes into connected writing. Compare with the transcripts in the Appendix, pp. 212 and 214, and check the answers to the questions.

Questions

Lecture on 'Marriage customs'.
1 What are the benefits of marriage for children?
2 What do you understand by the term *polyandry*?
3 What do you understand by *virilocal*, *uxorilocal* and *neolocal* marriage?
4 Briefly name the three possibilities about transfer of wealth in marriage.

Lecture on 'Computers'.
1 List three main areas of the application of computers to commerce and industry.
2 Give an example of a successful use of computers in information systems.
3 Give two examples of the use of the computer as an aid to design planning.
4 Why is it misleading to refer to computers as 'electronic brains'?

Group note taking

In spite of all the practice you have done in this unit, as a foreign student, you may still find occasionally that your comprehension of a lecture breaks down altogether. This may be because the lecturer speaks too quickly, or because you simply lose track of what he says. It is important that you should not give up when this happens: listen as intently as you can, jotting down a key word here and there. You will obviously also find it useful if there is a fellow student or group of students with whom you can literally 'compare notes' after a lecture. It would be helpful if there were one or more native speakers of English in the group. Discussion of 'What did he say?' may not only be useful for more complete notes, but also act as a kind of revision for everyone.

Preliminary topic

Exercise 1

Read through this passage. Your tutor will then lead a short class discussion.

As others see us

You remember that line of Robert Burns about seeing ourselves as others see us? I wonder how many of us have suddenly experienced that – have suddenly, as it were, been made to regard ourselves from outside, through the eyes, perhaps, of a foreign friend? I am not sure that the experience is wholly to be commended but let me give you two examples of what I mean.

An African chief, a man whom I had met in his own country in East Africa, came to England for the first time when he was well past sixty. He had never before left his own country – in which he held a high and responsible post – and he flew over here, rocketed as it were in a matter of hours from his own simple and familiar African surroundings to the complex and shifting crowds of London. A friend of mine went to call on him the morning after his arrival and asked him how he was and whether he was enjoying himself. The African chief said that he was feeling well, but he had had a frightening experience earlier that morning. He had gone, he said, to have a look round the streets and had found himself at Victoria Station. He said, 'Naturally I went in to see your trains. And I stood near some iron railings, by an iron gate, to watch a train come in and it was there that I saw this frightening thing. For, as the train came nearer and nearer to where I was standing, all the doors at one moment swung outward, and, while the train was still moving, a great many men jumped out, quite silently, and they began to run towards me. They carried umbrellas like spears, and their faces were set and unsmiling. I thought something terrible was about to happen, so I ran away.' Well, there it is. There is the 8.50 or the 9.15, or whatever your business train may be, arriving at a London station. And there we are, as this elderly African saw us, on his first day among us. The picture, mercifully, has its funny side, but, for me at any rate, the smile is mixed with slight unease. The next picture is even more searching. A girl visitor from Nigeria, fresh from the noisy, laughing fellowship of an African village, where greetings are everywhere and every house stands open, took lodgings in a London suburb. On her first

Sunday morning, she went for a walk with an English friend. The streets were unremarkable, empty and colourless: the doors of the houses closed, blinds drawn over many of the windows. When her friend, to whom all this was familiar, asked the Nigerian girl why she was shivering and silent, the girl said: 'It makes me feel afraid, it is like the city of the dead.'

Those are true stories. They have stuck in my mind because I have just returned to live in England after more than seven years in Africa, and those stories give me a glimpse of my country and my people through the eyes of two Africans meeting our society for the first time. I know that in a matter of weeks both of those Africans would be wonderfully at home here – for no people I have met have a greater power of adaptation than Africans. But those first impressions are valuable, as are the criticisms implied in them, because all that we stand for as people is now very much under criticism in a way it has not been before.

(From an article in *The Listener* by James Welch)

The purpose of seminars

A lot of teaching in colleges and universities is done with small groups of students: sometimes only four or five, perhaps ten or twelve, sometimes more. These small-group sessions are usually called *tutorials* or *seminars*. These words are loose terms which can mean different things in different places. In this unit, we shall use the term *seminar* for any type of small-group discussion.

Exercise 2

What advantages do seminars have over other methods of learning – e.g. attending lectures, reading in the library? Is there a particular kind of learning best done by seminar, and other kinds best done by attending lectures and reading? Discuss with your tutor.

Exercise 3

After your discussion make a list of the special advantages of learning by a) seminar, b) lecture, c) reading.

What happens in seminars

A seminar is a group activity. A successful seminar depends mainly on two things:
a) how the individual members of the group (the *participants*) behave.
b) how the group as a whole behaves.

Exercise 4

This exercise is concerned with the behaviour of individual participants. Participants' attitudes may be positive or negative. By *positive attitudes* we mean that an individual student has got a helpful way of thinking and behaving, which makes for a good discussion. *Negative attitudes*, on the other hand, are unhelpful attitudes. There are twenty ways of behaving listed below. Write down whether you think each attitude is positive or negative.

The student:
1   has previously thought about the topic.
2   is willing to listen to others.
3   never takes anything seriously.
4   is willing to change his opinion.
5   makes long speeches.
6   is not afraid to say what he believes.
7   will not give others a chance to speak.
8   will talk only to the tutor and not to other members of the group.
9   encourages other members of the group to speak.
10   makes sarcastic remarks.
11   is tolerant of others' beliefs.
12   makes his points concisely (briefly).
13   becomes angry or upset easily.
14   will support good ideas from other group members.
15   interrupts rudely.
16   pretends to agree with the rest of the group, although he really does not.
17   can relieve a tense or emotional situation with a joke.
18   shows that his own comments and ideas relate to points that previous speakers have made.
19   holds whispered conversations with his neighbour.
20   thinks that time spent on discussion is time wasted.

Exercise 5

Which statements apply to yourself? List them. Be honest!

Exercise 6

This exercise is concerned with how the group as a whole behaves. Below there is a list of ten factors which might affect the usefulness of a discussion. Write down whether you think each factor is positive (good, helpful) or negative (bad, unhelpful). *Note:* Some of these statements could be debated, and you could make your decision after discussion.

In a seminar:
1 everyone talks at the same time.
2 the group has clearly defined aims (i.e. it knows exactly what has to be decided etc).
3 there is a timetable for various stages of the discussion.
4 some participants take notes all the time and do not contribute to the discussion.
5 there is some time at the end for summing up and evaluation (i.e. deciding whether the discussion has been successful or not).
6 no-one takes any notes.
7 everyone contributes by saying something.
8 at the end, each student is aware of the opinions of the other members of the group.
9 most students leave the seminar with the same ideas and opinions that they came with.
10 mostly, the opinions that are expressed are supported by facts.

Exercise 7

Think of a recent discussion that you have attended or observed. Write down which of the statements in exercise 6 you think are true of that discussion. For some items, you may not be sure, and in that case put a query (?).

Exercise 8

It is very important to know *why* one is taking part in discussion. Below are some reasons that have been put forward for taking part in seminars. How important do you think they are? Indicate whether you think the reasons are very important, less important, or if you are not sure how important. If you can think of any more reasons, write them down. When you have finished, discuss your choices with the others in your group.

Reasons for having a seminar
1 It helps the students to understand the subject more deeply.
2 It improves students' ability to think.
3 It helps to solve a particular problem.
4 It helps the group to make a particular decision.
5 It gives you the chance to hear other students' ideas.
6 It improves students' English.
7 It increases students' confidence in speaking.
8 It changes students' attitudes.

The language of discussion

Usually the purpose of a seminar is to discuss ideas, not mainly to learn facts, although facts are important as evidence to support the ideas. When one of the other participants expresses an idea or opinion, you have to decide what your own thoughts are:

1 *You agree.* If so, do you agree completely, or do you think he is only partly right? Have you any arguments, facts etc which support the speaker's point of view?
2 *You disagree.* There is nothing wrong in disagreeing with a speaker. But always respect other people's views, and remember: you may be mistaken!
3 *You don't know.* You may be looking for more evidence, or you may not quite have understood what the speaker is trying to say.

Exercise 9

Here are some useful expressions for indicating whether you agree, disagree or don't know:

Agree
I couldn't agree more.
On the whole, I think the speaker's arguments are fair.

Disagree
I'm afraid I can't agree with Mr X on this matter.

Don't know
Is the speaker saying that . . .?
Am I correct in assuming . . .?

Under which heading would you put each of these expressions?

1 I'm sorry, I can't accept Mr X's point of view.
2 I think the speaker is right in what he says.
3 I'm afraid I'm not convinced.
4 I'm afraid I didn't quite get the speaker's last point. Could he go over it again, please?
5 All right. I take your point.
6 May I suggest another explanation?
7 Could I ask the speaker for his views on . . .
8 By and large, I would accept the speaker's views (but . . .)
9 I'm not sure that I entirely agree with Mr X.
10 Could I ask Mr X what he means by . . .

Exercise 10

Write down any other useful phrases with the same kind of meaning that you may come across.

Sometimes students do not know how to say that they would like *to come into the discussion*, or how to *interrupt* without giving offence. There are several phrases that can be used for this. Something else that you may like to do is to show that you have *changed your mind*, and now agree with something you disagreed with before. (It can happen!) You may also sometimes have to *sum up* what has been said.

Exercise 11

Below are some useful expressions for indicating that you want to *come into the discussion*, *change your mind* and *sum up*. Under which heading would you put each expression?

1 On reflection, I think that Mr X was perhaps right when he said . . .
2 I'd like to pick up one of the last speaker's points.
3 Could I come in at this point?
4 I'd like to withdraw what I said about . . .
5 The main points that have been made are . . .
6 Well, if I could just sum up the discussion, let me say . . .
7 Could I say something about . . .
8 Let me try to pull the main threads of this argument together.
9 I wonder if I could comment on that last point?
10 I think the members of the group are basically in agreement on the following points . . .

Exercise 12

Listen to people talking and write down other expressions that you hear with the same kind of meanings.

Various kinds of topics

A topic for discussion may be expressed in the form of a *statement* or a *question*. The subject matter of topics (that is, what they are about) may also take various forms. The most common are
1 Fact
2 Personal feeling
3 Opinion
4 Action

A lot of time is wasted in discussion because people confuse these four different kinds of topics. In fact, it is not always easy to see differences between them, but these differences will be explained in this section. This table shows suggested ways of handling the different kinds of topics:

Suggested ways of handling four different kinds of topics

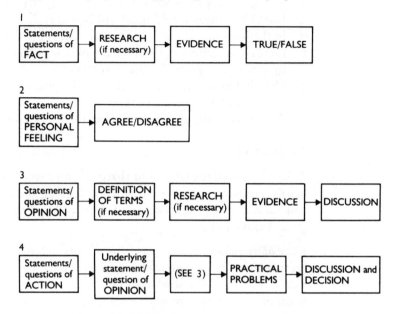

Statements/questions of fact

A statement of fact is a statement like:

'Brazil won the World Cup in 1958, 1962 and again in 1970.'

Similarly, a question of fact would be: 'Who won the World Cup in 1970?'

Statements of fact can be shown to be true or false. In other words, they can be *verified* by doing some *research*. (To verify something simply means to find out whether it is true or not.) The research will produce *evidence*. Sometimes, of course, there will be no evidence, or not enough evidence, to prove the matter either way, and then the matter has to be left until such time as enough evidence is found.

Exercise 13

Look at each of the following statements and say whether it is a statement of fact or not. Most of the answers are straightforward; a few you may want to discuss.

1   In 1971, the population of London (metropolitan area) was 7,379,014.

79

2   The south-east part of England is far too crowded.
3   The ideal length for a detective story is about 200 pages.
4   The theory of electromagnetic waves was originated by James Clerk Maxwell, the famous physicist.
5   Children should be more firmly disciplined in school.
6   The most common birds in Britain are the chaffinch and the blackbird: there are about ten million of each.
7   In the long run, country life is more satisfying than town life.
8   Increasing automation and the use of computers will lead to mass unemployment by the year 2000.
9   Certain kinds of pain can be relieved by acupuncture, i.e. using needles to pierce the skin.
10 At one time, the Earth was visited by beings from outer space.

Exercise 14

Take any one of the tables and charts in unit 2 (pp. 39–50) and briefly summarise a) what information it gives, and b) what conclusions may be drawn from it. You will find the vocabulary guide below useful.

Vocabulary guide

information	go to show
data	tend to show
findings	prove
results	demonstrate
tables	verify, verification
statistics	percentage
figures	median
proof	percentage
facts	source (of evidence etc)

Statements/questions of personal feeling

Exercise 15

Look at the following statements. For each statement say whether you *agree* or *disagree*. Is it possible to say whether the statements are *true* or *false*?

1 Coffee is a nicer drink than tea.
2 'People say that life is the thing, but I prefer reading' (Logan Pearsall Smith)
3 'God's masterpiece is a well-built woman' (Councilman Philip, Miami Beach City Council, quoted in the *Observer*)
4 'Anyone who hates children and dogs cannot be all bad' (W. C. Fields)

You may have agreed or disagreed with these statements, but it is not possible to *prove* that they are right or wrong, because they are *statements of personal feeling*. You will agree with them or not, depending on how you feel about coffee, reading, well-built women, children or dogs. Generally speaking, therefore, a statement/question of personal feeling is not a good seminar topic, although it may make a good *debating* topic where the object may be to entertain the listeners, rather than come to useful conclusions.

Exercise 16

Make a list of five statements of personal feeling. They could either be statements of your own, or statements made by someone else which you agree with. Find out how many of your friends agree with your statements. Remember that statements of personal feeling cannot be proved or verified.

Try introducing your statements with some of the expressions below.

Vocabulary guide

I feel	in my opinion
the way I see it	speaking personally
I think	speaking for myself

Statements/questions of opinion
Unlike statements/questions of personal feeling, statements/questions of opinion *can* be meaningfully disclosed, but they first of all require a) definition of terms, b) evidence.

Definition of terms
Do you agree with this opinion: 'Women are better drivers than men'? You may say that you cannot answer until you know what is meant by 'better drivers'. This phrase could mean:
a) safer drivers
b) faster drivers
c) more courteous drivers
d) more cautious drivers
e) more interested in machines.

Perhaps someone who agrees with this opinion means all of these things, or some of them, or something else entirely. There is no point in having a discussion if the people taking part are talking about different things. It may be necessary, therefore, for the members of a group to *define their terms* before they can start a discussion: in other words, to say exactly what they mean.

Exercise 17

Look at the following statements/questions of opinion. Underline any terms (i.e. words or phrases) which you think might have to be defined before a meaningful discussion can take place.

1 Is democracy the best way of running a country?
2 President Kennedy was probably the greatest American president of modern times.
3 Scientists should be allowed to perform any kind of experiment they like; otherwise progress will come to a halt.
4 In this day and age, no-one can consider himself truly educated unless he has studied a scientific subject.
5 The urban (city) way of life is obviously an unnatural way of life, and that is another reason why country people should be discouraged from moving to the towns.
6 I think that everyone will agree that the first duty of the government is to ensure that every worker gets a fair wage.
7 The highest wages ought to be paid to those who actually do the work – in other words, the members of the working class.
8 Scotland ought to have its freedom, like any other nation.

Exercise 18

Take any two of the above statements and discuss the different things which the underlined words or phrases could mean.

Vocabulary guide

ambiguous	have several possible meanings/interpretations
vague	one possible meaning
confusing	one interpretation
puzzling	one way/another way of defining . . . could be . . .
confused by	I would interpret . . . to mean . . .
puzzled by	My interpretation of . . . is . . .

Evidence

Usually, a person who puts forward an opinion should be able to back it up, to support it, with *evidence*. We have already seen that by evidence we mean *facts* which can be *verified*. Let us look again at this opinion: 'Women are better drivers than men'. Let us imagine that the group has discussed the definition of 'better drivers', and has agreed that 'better drivers' = 'safer drivers'.

Exercise 19

Say how useful the following kinds of evidence would be in a discussion of this kind:
a) one member of the group knows a woman driver who is very

82

careless and forgetful.

b) the percentage of women drivers and men drivers found guilty of dangerous driving in a recent year (the two percentages to be compared).

c) the number of claims that women drivers make on their car insurance companies as compared to men drivers.

We can see that a) is an example of evidence based on a person's experience (sometimes called *anecdotal evidence*). Sometimes this kind of evidence is acceptable and sometimes not. On the other hand b) and c) are examples of *statistical evidence*, which is more usually acceptable.

Exercise 20

Look at the following statements of opinion. What kind of evidence would be useful for a discussion of these topics?

1 Governments all over the world will have to pass laws to limit the number of children in each family; otherwise, there will be mass-starvation by the year 2000.
2 Smoking cigarettes is bad for your health.
3 All drivers should be forced to wear seat-belts when they are driving their cars.
4 Hanging is a deterrent to murder (i.e. some murders would not be committed if the murderers knew they would be hanged if caught).
5 When workers strike the reason given for the strike is usually a wage claim of some kind. But the real reason for most strikes is boring and unpleasant working conditions.
6 Students attending universities now are less left-wing and less opposed to authority than they were ten years ago.

Vocabulary guide (see also exercise 14)

positive correlation (e.g. 'There is a positive correlation between intelligence and success in study: more intelligent students are generally more successful.')

negative correlation (e.g. 'There is a negative correlation between laziness and success in study: lazy students are generally less successful.')

correlate with

correspond with

tend to show

trend

tendency

compare

comparison

Statements/questions of action

Look at these statements/questions:

1 We ought to make all schools comprehensive (i.e. all children should go to the same local secondary school, regardless of ability).

2 Should all major industries in a country be nationalised (i.e. taken over by the government)?

3 Let's have a party at the end of term.

You can see that in all of these statements or questions, some kind of *action* is suggested.

A statement/question of action usually has two elements underlying it:

a) A statement/question of *opinion*. If I say, 'Let us do X' or 'Let us abolish Y', then I must believe that 'X is a good thing' or 'Y is a bad thing'. In the same way, if I say 'Should we do X?', I may be asking 'Is X a good thing?'

b) A *practical* element. How is X to be done? For example, everyone may agree that it would be a good idea to have a party at the end of term, but there may still be practical problems, such as who is to arrange it, whether we can afford it etc.

So most discussions of statements/questions of action should take place in two stages:

i) does the group agree with the underlying statement/question of opinion?

ii) if the answer is 'yes', are there any practical problems? How can they be overcome?

Exercise 21

Choose one or more of the following topics. Assume that your group has agreed that the action that is suggested is a good thing. What are the *practical* problems involved? Have you any suggestions about how they could be solved?

1 We ought to make all schools comprehensive.

2 All major industries should be nationalised.

3 All factories and businesses should be run by workers' councils, elected by ordinary workers.

4 Private wealth should be abolished.

5 Everyone should be paid the same wage, irrespective of the job he does.

6 There ought to be a World Government.

7 Examinations should be abolished.

8   Universities should be open to anyone who wants to attend
    them.
9   Esperanto (an artificial language) should be adopted as the
    international means of communication.
10 Instead of just locking up criminals in cells, we should make
    them repay their debt to society by doing something useful.

Vocabulary guide

complication	awkward
difficulty	impossible
handicap	problematic
obstacle	complicate (matters)
problem	make things difficult
in a dilemma	make (it) impossible (to)
answer	find the key to
key	solve
solution	find a way round (a difficulty)
	overcome (a difficulty)
	resolve (a problem)

Seminar practice

This section consists of a series of brief statements putting forward
a point of view. The statements are views which have been
expressed in the form of letters or articles appearing in *The
Sunday Times*. Each topic may be dealt with in the following
way:

Before the discussion:
1 One member of the group (the *presenter*) prepares a very brief
   summary of the topic, and notes down his own point of view.
   (He may also do some research on his own.)
2 The other members of the group read the topic and make a
   note of three or four points which they may raise. (They may
   also do some research.)

At the beginning of the discussion:
1 The presenter gives his summary and his own views (5–7
   minutes).
2 The discussion proceeds.

At the end of the discussion:
The group evaluates the discussion.

Exercise 22

Topic: Is there a connection between television programmes and the amount of violence today?

Academics challenge report on children and TV violence

A NEW study claiming to document a connection between violence on television and violence in real life is already coming under attack from academics. They say that the author is demanding action on his report before producing detailed findings to substantiate it.

Dr William Belson told the British Association for the Advancement of Science in Birmingham last week that his research suggested that boys exposed to high levels of television violence were 50 per cent more likely to commit acts of violence than boys who had not been exposed.

His £110,000 survey, paid for by CBS, the American television company, studied more than 1,500 London boys aged between 12 and 16. He closed his paper with a call for immediate action on his recommendations to reduce levels of TV violence and specific kinds of violence which he claimed were more damaging than others. His recommendations were enthusiastically endorsed by Mrs Mary Whitehouse.

Social scientists familiar with the field have a number of specific queries about Belson's work. They point out that a statistical technique invented by him and central to his research has been criticised by some academics in the past. Robin McCron, of the Mass Communications Research Centre at Leicester University, says, 'Self reporting—asking the subject to give his own account of the evidence—is notoriously unreliable. Studies have put the possible error as high as 20 per cent, and we don't know what checks there were in this work. The fact that Belson paid the boys may have had an influence. Without the full data, it can't be checked.'

McCron adds: 'His questions on the programmes go back 12 years. If the boys were aged between 13 and 16 it means the oldest was only four years old when the first programmes were broadcast. How reliable is the memory of a child that young likely to be on the programmes he watched? Dr Belson may have answers, but we just don't know.'

The Nelson affair highlights the difficulties faced by researchers into television violence—problems so severe that at least one British group has withdrawn from the field completely. 'It's impossible to do serious scientific work in this area now,' says Robin McCron. 'It has moved out of the academic world and it has been taken over by pressure groups and politics.'

Indeed, experience in television research in America reveals how treacherous this field has become. Results of nervous projects there have been found, at worst, contradictory, at best, inconclusive.

(From an article by Isabel Hilton)

Mrs Mary Whitehouse: a well-known campaigner against the low standards of morality which she says are to be found in British TV programmes.

Exercise 23

Topic: Can one make too many sacrifices for excellence in sport?

Dick Marcroft took up judo at 23, too late to get to the top. Now, at 39, he is Southern Area Coach and chief coach at his local club in Tonbridge, Kent. 'If I had started judo at eight I would have got myself into the British team,' he says. Instead he has driven himself and his proteges with savage dedication: 'Now I've produced four internationals, two of them my sons and one my nephew.'

His son Andrew and nephew Martin, are both members of the 16-18 British judo squad. His younger son, Jeremy, is, at 15, in the national boys' squad.

'Jeremy is going through what we have been through and I feel sorry for him,' says Andrew. Looking at Dick, Martin says quietly. 'There were times when we have really hated you.' Andrew adds, 'I have been fighting on the mat as hard as I could and he always wanted more than I had got to give, I used to think, I hate you, I'll get you when I'm older.'

His father simply nods. 'They have often wanted to give up, but I put pressure on them. Told them they had put in years and could get further still.'

Dick's wife, Marion, says: 'I often said it was time it all finished, it was too much. When they came back from hard competitions he would make them work again and I wished they had never started judo. We had rows about it, I tried to stop it, but I never had much of a say.'

The boys have done well in competitions, almost from the first local contests. But in 1976 Martin and his parents began counting the cost. His mother, Vivien explains: 'He had been coming in from training and starting revision at 11.30 at night. He failed all his exams, although everyone said he was pretty bright.' Martin is now working as an office clerk, regret-ting the studies he has missed, Andrew is an apprentice garage mechanic; both are 17.

Has it been worth all the hard work, the back injuries and torn ligaments? 'I think it has done them good,' said Dick. 'We bring our children up too soft in this country. If they hadn't been judo players they would have been hanging around with friends, drinking, smoking, and perhaps getting into trouble.

'They were nothing special when they started judo at eight, but any eight-year-old can get to the top—if parents push them and they are prepared to be pushed.'

Did the boys have a real choice, could Andrew have dropped out?

'Any time, but there would have been a packed suitcase at the bottom of the stairs and a sign saying This Way Out,' he says.

'Too right', adds Dick.

MARTIN MARCROFT'S 1977 EXPENSES

Petrol	£600·00
Spending money at training	£50·00
Spending money on trips	£242·00
Entry fees	£60·00
Equipment	£97·00
Club fees	£40·00
Special food	£72·00
Companion's costs	£25·00
TOTAL	**£1186**

Help: when abroad with British team, travel and accommodation paid.

Weekly training time: 13 hours plus competitions and travelling and additional training before competitions.

Exercise 24

Topic: Should bars and pubs in Britain be open longer?

Cheer up, not close up

THERE IS a time for many things —Sunday, for instance, for the *Sunday Times*. But there is no such natural rhythm to man's desire for a drink. At this time of year we enviously recall sunny days in Spain or France when we could summon a drink just when we wanted it. But not here, where Puritanism is enforced by an unholy alliance between the temperance lobby and the pub trade.

It is time that Parliament enacted the recommendations of the Erroll committee, whose report has already mouldered through three Governments. Erroll said the present limits, which are no more than a relic of First World War austerity, should be eased so that, with certain safeguards, pubs and bars could be open at any time between 10 am and midnight. They need not be open all the time but could suit themselves or rather, for a change, their customers.

There is no evidence that such an extension would increase drunkenness. Recent Scottish experience points the opposite way. Here is something that a political party could put in its manifesto at no cost to the taxpayer and at no sacrifice of political principle. Let them compete, for once, to offer us some cheer.

temperance lobby: group of people who wish to see the sale of liquor restricted or abolished.
Recent Scottish experience: the times for opening bars etc in Scotland have been made much more flexible than they used to be.

Extra drinking time a risk

I AM worried by your leader last week which urged that Parliament should enact the recommendations of the Erroll report to ease the present licensing hours.

There may be no natural rhythms to man's desire to drink, but there are social and occupational rhythms. Our recollections of France and Spain are coloured by being tourists. Perceptive citizens of those countries would find such freely available alcohol a source of grave concern.

Alcohol is a dangerous drug and it is not only puritans and the temperance lobby that are concerned with the damage it does. Alcoholism is on the increase in this country. Its incidence ultimately depends on the total quantity of alcohol consumed by our society. This depends, among other things, on availability. This is in turn related to licensing hours.

Alcoholism must not be confused with drunkenness (intoxication). Many of those who get drunk are not alcoholics. Conversely many alcoholics are rarely intoxicated in public.

Intoxication depends on the dose of alcohol (i.e. the quantity drunk in a given time). This quantity depends on custom, habit and price for any given individual. If the time available for drinking is restricted then there may be an increased risk of intoxication. Conversely if drinking time is extended then the chances of intoxication could be reduced.

However if licensing hours are unduly prolonged then customs and habits change and the total quantity of alcohol consumed will go up with an increase in alcoholism. While there is a need to reduce intoxication the priority is to avoid alcoholism.

D. H. MARJOT
Consultant-in-charge
Regional Alcoholism and
Drug Dependence Unit
St Bernard's Hospital
Southall

Exercise 25

Topic: Is the use of nuclear power the answer to Britain's fuel problems?

Nuclear power cuts pollution

TWENTY-FIVE years ago many families were satisfied with a home that had only one electric socket. Such a house would also commonly have had no hot water supply. The electric wiring would not have been designed to accept any load greater than a single-bar heater. Indeed, older houses had electric lighting downstairs only. Living standards have risen; what were once considered to be reasonably comfortable homes are now unacceptable for even the poorest families.

These improved standards have increased the demand for electricity. After falling when prices rose in 1973, electricity consumption is again increasing with the domestic market as its biggest single user. The National Grid now supplies over 230m 'units' of electricity every year. More than 70 per cent comes from ordinary coal-fired power stations.

I live near one of these stations at Willington in the Trent valley. According to the CEGB's booklet about Willington, its capacity is 804 megawatts (it isn't one of the larger power stations) and it produces 9,000 tons of solid waste every week of full output. The booklet doesn't mention airborne effluents, but they're probably much the same as those reported from America in 1968 by the US Bureau of Radiological Health and the US Office of Science and Technology. These reports say that an 800-megawatt station discharges more than 3,000 tons of gaseous sulphur dioxide to the atmosphere a week. It also discharges, by the way, over 400 tons of nitrogen peroxide and carbon monoxide, as well as enough particulate radium to produce radioactive fall-out somewhat greater than that around a nuclear power station.

It's the solid wastes and sulphur dioxide that are the really urgent problems, as there's no way at present of coping with waste products on this scale. Scientists are investigating improved methods of burning coal, but these improved techniques won't make any significant difference in less than 15 years. Meanwhile each existing power station will add thousands of tons more pollutants to the environment in every week. These pollutants are a proven health hazard; in unfavourable circumstances they can be mass killers. One hundred and fifty children were killed by solid wastes at Aberfan; the village of Trehafod was evacuated in 1976 for fear of a similar disaster. Four thousand died of bronchial troubles in the 1952 London smog. Subsequent Clean Air legislation has reduced visible smoke, but the level of acidic gases has increased.

Perhaps renewable natural energy sources will eventually take over from coal-fired plant. But it won't happen in this century. The technologies aren't yet ready. It would take a thousand of the largest windmills ever built

—or a wave-energy barrage so long that it won't fit across the Straits of Dover—to replace just one coal-burning power station. In fact, nuclear power is the only alternative source that can do anything to reduce pollution within the next two decades.

The CEGB's next nuclear power station will be commissioned at Heysham. If it isn't available for any reason, it will be replaced by keeping 1200 megawatts of obsolete coal-fired plant on line—there's no practical alternative. When the Heysham station is working at full output it will discharge in a week, on average, about 30 pounds of solid waste, no toxic gases and less radioactivity than a coal-fired station. And remember, there's no positive evidence of even one person dying from the radioactivity of a nuclear power station during the whole history of our nuclear industry.

But, if the Heysham station is delayed for just one year, a further 196,000 tons of sulphur dioxide will be added to the atmosphere and another 560,000 tons of solid wastes will pile up in our overburdened environment.

(From an article by Rowland Pocock, Nuclear Engineer)

bronchial troubles: illness associated with breathing; chest complaints.
smog: combination of smoke and fog.
CEGB: Central Electricity Generating Board (main authority in Britain supervising the generation/production of electricity).

Exercise 26

Topic: Does heavy taxation stop people from working hard?

Tax cuts with pink stamps

IT IS debatable whether a significant number of people in Britain today would work harder or more effectively if their take-home pay were increased by the cuts in income tax canvassed by Tories and Liberals in amendments to the Finance Bill. Incentives are a grey area only measurable when you have crossed it, but the presumption must be that lower taxes would help. It is indisputable that if our present system of taxing all incomes above the lowest at high and ultimately crushing rates continues more people will work less hard and less effectively, save by moonlight. Blue collar dishonesty and white collar crime are unlikely to breed a healthy economy.

All political parties, it appears, now agree that this is so. They would be even more obtuse than the electors believe them to be if they didn't. In his 'think again' letter to the Chancellor of the Exchequer last week, John Greenborough, president of the Confederation of British Industry, put the case as dispassionately as anyone could.

'You have said that the key to growth and high employment must lie in an improvement of Britain's industrial performance. We agree. But the Budget as it now stands will not achieve this objective. It is, in effect, a tax on skill . . . As you yourself have recognised, the acquisition of skills and incentives and the acceptance of greater responsibility need to be made much more attractive than at present. Yet by giving much smaller benefits proportionately to the skilled than to the unskilled your proposals will do exactly the opposite.'

The Budget poll conducted by MORI for *The Sunday Times* showed that 73% agreed (only 22% disagreed) 'that higher paid people pay so much tax that there is no incentive for them to work harder.' Among members of trade unions the split was 70%-21%; among Conservatives, 84%-15%; and among Labour supporters, 65%-30%.

(From an article by Kenneth Fleet)

pink stamps: trading stamps given to purchaser of goods; may be exchanged without payment for articles provided by trading stamp firm.

the Finance Bill: bill put before the House of Commons to change taxes etc.

by moonlight: by taking on extra work in addition to one's normal job.

blue collar/white collar: manual workers/clerical workers.

dispassionately: unemotionally.

incentives: things that encourage people to do work.

MORI: an opinion-poll organisation.

No incentive

LAST SUNDAY, while Kenneth Fleet said that 'the presumption must be that lower taxes' would help to get people to 'work harder or more effectively,' your leader went bashing on with the claim that the cost of reducing taxes on middle and higher incomes 'would be recovered in increased industrial activity.' How do you know? Has there been some research to prove your statement?

Selwyn Lloyd in 1961 reduced taxes on higher incomes specifically as an incentive for exporters. Each surtax-payer gained a minimum of £500, probably worth £1,500 in today's money. I don't recall that this was followed by our flooding Japan with Rolls-Royces, or indeed, flooding anywhere with anything.

C. WILLIAMSON
Blackpool

Topic: Should very seriously ill people only die naturally or should a doctor or the person himself be allowed to choose the time of death?

Life and death:
Each man should face his own

AS I LAY in Charing Cross Hospital, I read Martin Williams's article (Opinion last week). I, too, am having treatment for cancer and, at 28, I have now had two operations, some 10 weeks of radiotherapy and nine months of chemotherapy, described by Hubert Humphrey as 'bottled death' (I see it as bottled life).

I may yet die but expect to be cured and remain optimistic in a country which seems totally pessimistic — there are grounds for optimism but people don't seem to want to see them.

People expect you to die and because of their own inability to face their own deaths, they feel you also will be unable to cope. However, I have found the fear of pain worse than the fear of death. Both are personal and can only be dealt with on a personal level but it is wrong to imply that there is no help available. We do the medical profession a disservice if we imply this. Everybody at Charing Cross, from experienced consultants to recently-qualified house doctors and young nurses has been extremely helpful and made coping easier.

If I die I feel confident that they will allow me to do this in my own way and I know they will be a help to me. All I ask is that we should not expect them to face our own disasters for us whether that be death or a painful illness.

LEONARD ROBINSON
Tadworth

RARE EXAMPLES: Derek Humphrey's account in his book *Jean's Way* of the manner in which he fulfilled his promise to aid his wife to die on her own terms, as an alternative to a lingering death, and Baroness Wootton's article 'The Right Way to Die' are rare published examples of a rational approach to death.

More consideration is now given to the whole subject of dying than hitherto but, deplorably, so far Parliament has not established the individual's inherent right to die at will other than by suicide. Members of the Criminal Law Revision Committee are seeking the means of changing the law to make mercy killing at worst a minor offence, providing it is 'with the consent or without the dissent of the deceased'.

'Mercy killing' is unfortunately a misleading term; it is the disease or body disorder which is the killer, therefore merciful release is the better term.

Nevertheless, quite apart from the requisite mental and moral calibre, it is not only reasonable, but it is humane to dissociate relatives from any part in the practice of euthanasia. This is not only to avoid suspicion of mixed motives, but also because of the more usual and natural surge of emotion which would make purely objective decisions most difficult in such times of distress, and perhaps leave a lingering sense of guilt or doubt, especially where the patient is comatosed or confused by mental impairment.

The real need is for voluntary euthanasia to be legalised to enable adults who so wish, to ensure, by a prior declaration in writing, that the end of their life shall be gentle and dignified as set out by Baroness Wootton.

CHARLES WILSHAW
London, N.12

---

inherent: within us; not caused or controlled by other people.

euthanasia: the merciful killing of people, e.g. to save them from suffering.

Exercise 28

Topic: Is homework useless?

Useless homework

HOMEWORK is like a treasured old complaint that has been uncomfortably aching for 30 years in my memory and must have caused misery for much longer than that. It is what teachers complain is not done, or not done tidily or carefully. It is what teachers complain gives them mountains of exercise books to carry from home to school and from school to home and so on ad infinitum.

It is what prevents teachers preparing their lessons. It is what children do hurriedly on buses. It is what parents can no longer help their children with because they do not understand modern methods. It is what causes exercise books and text books to be lost and become dog-eared. In an age of leisure it is what can have adolescent children working in solitary rooms till 10 or 11 p.m. while their parents watch television.

On any measure, used as a general method, it can probably be shown to be educationally counter-productive. Because it is so frequently not done it weakens the authority of the school and the teacher. Because it is often done hurriedly and without the teacher's supervision it is often badly presented and erroneous. Worst of all it is not always corrected, and what could diminish motivation more? It actually interferes with teaching because the rituals of setting, handing back, commenting on, collecting marks, preparing for the next piece of homework can well occupy the whole teaching space available and appear to be what education is all about.

There is everything to be said for children being able to learn at home as well as at school, for parents to be involved and for children being able to use educational facilities outside the school and use the school's equipment beyond school time. There is also everything to be said for separating out times when children work individually from times when they are being taught. But this need not lead to the largely useless nightly ritual of tens of millions of books being transported from schools to homes—pupils' and teachers'.

Putting individual work by children into the day's timetable would alter the school curriculum a good deal, and I think a good deal for the better. The corrective part of marking could take place while teachers, and pupils are together. It should improve the quality of work and still leave ample room for individual and exciting projects. It ought to make teachers think more clearly about their pedagogy. It ought to enable us to make a lot more sense of modern schooling. Above all, it might

93

make the school more of a modern workplace. In industry, the most effective administrators do not take their work home.

(From an article by Alex McGuire)

dog-eared: frayed and torn at the edges.
counter-productive: hindrance rather than help.

Reply from the workface

DISCIPLINE: As a 15 year-old working to take nine O-levels this summer and undergoing the rigours of two to three hours homework most nights, I feel Alex MacGuire's system offers many advantages. However, I would ask him to think of the effects of putting this system into practice.

Homework is not only work to be done at home. It is handing over responsibility from the teacher to the child, saying 'It is up to you now.' It is very easy to do it hastily or not at all. The only way a child learns to discipline himself or herself to do work he probably does not like is by doing it at home. If 'homework' was done at school in special periods this important development of self-discipline would be lost.

JOSEPHINE STEADMAN
Willaston, Wirral, Merseyside

Exercise 29

Topic: What is the most important thing in making a job satisfying?

A place to go between weekends

ASKED about the level of their own job satisfaction people nearly always have a clear memory of someone they met once who was totally satisfied and whose image has stuck in their minds. Occasionally, it sounds like a rather mythical figure—the craftsman building a dry stone wall, or the house painter who refused to knock off.

For themselves most people at least aim to strike a tolerable balance between earning enough to stay at a certain social level and a fairly congenial place to go between weekends. An excessively large part of the workforce is acknowledged to be stuck somewhere below this basic level of personal satisfaction.

With pay-rises slowed down but tax still running strongly, more and more people have been thinking about what they get out of their jobs apart from a salary or a pay-packet. Or at least, trying to think. Part of the trouble is—as we found in a sampling of people in a variety of occupations—that jobs become habitual and people do not register that there might be ways of improving things until their ideas are jogged by a questionnaire. While some of our sample complained of tax as the big obstacle to work-pleasure, it was the Inland Revenue man himself—rather bored with the monotony of his case-load—who strongly urged that everyone should get down

94

to hard study of job satisfaction.

Some kinds of worker, as in the entertainment industry, find it hard to admit publicly that they are not always having a wonderful time. But it is an area of genuine acceptance of poor and risky pay on the way up for the sake of the moments of fulfilment out on the boards. Joe Loss, the band leader, still going strong at 68, says he feels very lucky to have found a job that suited him so well. 'The irregular and long hours a band works when it's on the road would terrify some people, and the pay has been really low. But applause still excites me and I'd do it all again.'

Mike Yarwood of more recent vintage, echoes the enthusiasm. 'Being a comedian is easily the best job anyone could have. You avoid thinking about how precarious it is.'

Showbiz people are hard ones to follow on job satisfaction. But social workers, clergymen, and some nurses come close to it in their different way. They distil job satisfaction into an even neater spirit since they can almost never look forward to any glittering prizes. The main point made by our social worker in South London was that his job satisfaction would be much increased, and frustrations eased, if only he were given more resources to spend. He did not mention his own pay.

Surprisingly perhaps to those who do not have much of it, a sense of public duty is a genuine job satisfier even in echelons which look largely commercial or just well-paid. Peter Parker, chairman of British Rail, says it is a big part of the reward for his work. Doing your job to the exclusion of all other interests, he thinks, is highly destructive of personality and a dis-satisfier in the end.

Down among the poorest paid jobs the satisfactions get more subtle and hard for the outsider to understand. An attendant in a below-pavement public 'Gents' admitted that an eight-hour shift could be the height of tedium for £45 a week take-home pay. But he liked it because it was an easy number, he got to know a few friendly faces, and he was his own boss, in a manner of speaking. Also 'It's ten times better than I felt when I was unemployed.'

(From an article by Roy Perrot and Patricia James)

Exercise 30

Topic: Should all professional people do a spell of manual work from time to time?

Discovering truth down among the workers

SHATTERING: While looking for my first teaching post, I took a job as a packer at a London store. The experience of being a mere worker was shattering. The frustration of being treated as an imbecile is beyond description. After a few months I achieved the dizzy heights of stock-controller, changed my overall from brown to white and obtain-ed my own desk, but the boredom of doing a simple job over and over again was a constant nightmare.

All the people I worked with could have performed their tasks blindfolded, but management had to tell them how to do them. This led to a sense of bitter irony when it became clear that management had no idea even how to start on these tasks.

After nine weeks in my present job, as a building site

labourer, I fully agree with Martin Leighton that 'unskilled' workers are some of the most skilled workers one can come across, turning their hand to anything and making a good job of it. But again they are dogged with a disease called management, which asks for one thing and then changes its mind.

R. M. HARRIS
Strensall, York

NON-PERSON: I quit a position as a junior executive with a property company and took a job in a plastics factory. I worked from 8 a.m. to 8 p.m. with an hour (unpaid) for lunch and no other breaks. As a 'trainee extrusion machine setter' one was totally occupied in running one's machine. To visit the lavatory one had to catch the eye of a supervisor, who would take over for a couple of minutes. You didn't operate the machines, they operated you. How very real the feeling of being a non-person was to me!

GEOFF GEORGE
St Sampsons, Guernsey

CONTACT: While at university I took a number of vacation jobs. To a nicely-brought-up girl from an academic family, the horror of sitting at a conveyor-belt for eight hours a day packing chocolate buttons was indescribable. I also remember the feeling of being a non-person as a tea-lady to the managers and secretaries of a small firm.

I hope the custom of students doing manual labour continues. For many of us it is the first time we have been in close contact as equals with members of the working class.

CATHERINE ASHER
Cramlington

DIFFICULT: As a managing director of a specialist construction company, I suggest that Martin Leighton's experience is not typical. He went into jobs where the interview was minimal, which indicates that the organisations concerned were not particularly careful to fit the individual to the role. I would like to suggest that Mr Leighton tries to be a manager. He will find out what a difficult job it is, and that mix-ups and mistakes occur because a manager is trying to deal with what is going to happen in the future as well as what is happening now.

A. R. L. CARR
Walton-on-the-Hill, Surrey

HOURS: Very few of the plumbers, electricians and painters who have come to my house have arrived before 9 a.m. and none have stayed after 4 p.m. They use my phone, drink innumerable cups of my coffee and tea—and have always left something behind, which they have to go back to the 'yard' for. My GP husband goes off at 8 a.m. and often doesn't come in at night till 10.30 p.m. Don't talk to us about the working classes!

MRS PAMELA DE LAUNAY
Kingston-on-Thames

GP: general practitioner (family doctor).

Further topics

Here are some more topics you can discuss. This time you will
have to do all the research and preparation of ideas yourself.

1 City life has been a failure – everyone should return to the
   country.
2 The tourist industry should be discouraged.
3 Experiments on animals are wrong and should be made
   illegal.
4 No family should be allowed to have more than two children.
5 Co-education is a good thing.
6 The profit motive (that is, doing things only for money) is
   immoral and unnecessary.
7 All important industries and services should be run by the
   State.
8 Corporal punishment (that is, punishment using a belt, cane
   etc.) should not be allowed in schools.
9 Examinations should be replaced by some other form of
   assessment.
10 Changes in fashion are simply a way of getting people to
   spend more money.

Unit 5   Writing an essay   i) Research and using the library

The importance of essays

In many university and college courses these days, the tendency is for the traditional type of formal examination at the end of the term or academic year to become less important. The emphasis is more on work that the student does more or less on his own *during* the course. These pieces of written work are usually called *essays*. A long piece of work for higher degrees is called a *dissertation* or *thesis*. In this unit, we shall call any piece of written work an *essay*.

Exercise 1

What do you think is the better way of finding out about a student's progress: examinations or essays? Are they both necessary? What are the qualities that a student has to have to do well in examinations? What are the qualities that he has to have to do well in essays? Make a list of your answers to the last two questions.

Systems for tackling essays

In spite of the importance of essays in a student's work, it is surprising how many students do not seem to be aware of certain elementary techniques in writing essays, and so get poorer grades than they could have got. Of course, writing essays cannot be made easy: any worthwhile piece of work demands time and thought. But sometimes essays get less credit than they could because they have not been researched well enough, or because they have been properly organised or presented.

A student can save himself a lot of time and effort, and perhaps earn himself better grades as well, by having a *system* for tackling essays.

In this unit we shall concentrate on essays for which background reading is necessary. We shall discuss two programmes for tackling such essays in a systematic way:

98

programme 1 deals with writing an essay using your tutors' references, programme 2 your own references.

Programme 1 : using your tutor's references

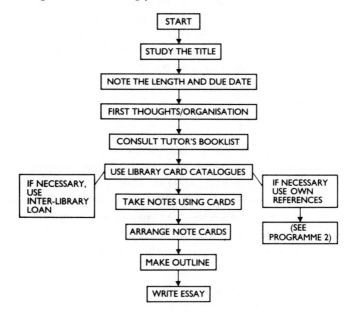

Programme 2: using your own references

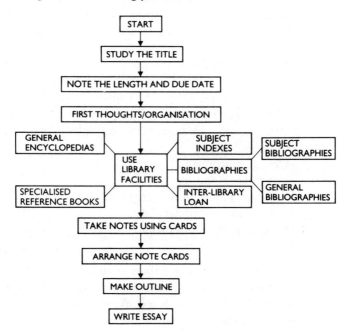

Exercise 2

Look carefully through the two programmes. Beside each box put:

✓ if you normally do what is mentioned in the box (you should at least put a tick beside the first and last boxes!)

X if you do not normally do what is mentioned in the box.

? if you do not understand what is being referred to in the box. (Be honest with yourself!)

START

You should start by finding out how important the essay is. This means that you should know where this particular essay fits into the course as a whole. How many essays will you be expected to write on this subject? What is the *weighting* of the essay (i.e. how many marks is it worth)? How many other essays will you have to do this term in all your subjects? This will help you to decide how much time you can afford to spend on this particular essay.

STUDY THE TITLE

The titles of essays are very important. Many students have worked very hard on an essay but got very little credit for it, because they have not understood the title. If you are in doubt about the meaning of a title, always check with your tutor. He should certainly clear up anything that is ambiguous (i.e. not clear). On the other hand, do not think that he is being unhelpful if he does not go into too much detail. He may wish you to think through the topic for yourself and work out your own approach.

Titles of essays are basically of two kinds: a) general titles b) specific titles. Here are some examples of *general titles*:
Democracy today
Marriage customs
The origins of speech
The development of the aeroplane
Technology and modern life
The Middle Ages in Europe
Rockets and space travel

The first thing to notice about such titles is that they are very *broad in scope*. If you choose the topic for your research it is usually best to make the topic as specific as possible, otherwise you may find it difficult to do justice to it.

Exercise 3

Look again at the list of general titles. One of the titles is 'Technology and modern life'. By *technology* we mean, of course, the use of science for practical purposes, e.g. the development of the motor-car, electrical goods and services and so on. So a more *specific* title in the same area would be 'Traffic conditions in modern cities'. Take any three of the titles given and see if you can think of a more specific title in the same area.

NOTE THE LENGTH AND DUE DATE

This is why the *length* of the essay is important. Most students (quite naturally) are interested in the recommended length of an essay because it gives them an idea of how much work they have to do! But the length is also related to the title. For example, if you are asked to write 2000 words on 'Marriage customs', then you cannot be expected to deal with the subject in depth.

The due date (i.e. the date when the essay should be handed in) is also important because sometimes you can be given a lower grade for not submitting work on time, even though you may have taken more time in order to do a better job.

Titles and topics

When you are given a general title, one of two things may be required: either a) you are expected to give some sort of survey of the topic; or b) you are expected to choose some particular aspect of it and deal with it in some detail.

In a survey answer you might have to say something briefly about each of the various aspects of the topic. In a detailed answer you would select one topic and write about that. Usually you will know what kind of answer is required but if in doubt, ask your tutor.

So, for one reason or another, you should train yourself in breaking general topics into sub-topics.

Exercise 4

Here are some very general titles. Write down *five* possible sub-topics contained within each title.
General topic
1 Agriculture and the modern world
2 Education yesterday and today
3 Advertising
4 The criminal and society

Exercise 5

Write down the title of two subjects that your specialise in or are interested in. Then write down five or six of the main divisions of the subject.

Your own ideas

FIRST THOUGHTS/ORGANISATION

You have thought carefully about the title of your essay and the scope of the topic you intend to write about. The next thing is to note down your first thoughts about the topic, *before you start reading it up*.

It may be that the title you have been given means absolutely nothing to you, and so you have no ideas about it at all. In that case you will have to start doing your research very quickly!

Mostly, however, you have some ideas about the essay that has been given to you. If that is the case, note these ideas down. There are at least two reasons for doing this.

Firstly, it is wise to be clear about your own position on a topic before you start reading what the 'experts' say. This does not mean that your views are correct and theirs are wrong. Often, the opposite is true. Nevertheless, you *may* be right, and you should not readily adopt someone else's views unless you are sure that his views are correct. On the other hand, don't be stubborn: be open to the ideas of others who may have thought about the subject more deeply than you.

Another reason for jotting down your own ideas is that your outlook becomes more comprehensive. You may think of aspects of the topic which are not covered in the texts that have been recommended to you.

Exercise 6

Imagine that you have to write an essay on the topic 'Should capital punishment be part of the legal system in a civilised society?' Your tutor has given you some books to read, but before doing so you want to be clear in your mind what your own ideas on this subject are.

1 Take a sheet of paper and divide it into two halves, putting on one side the heading *Yes* and on the other side the heading *No*. Decide which answer to the question you agree with and put a circle round it.

2 Underneath the heading you have circled make a list of the arguments which support your point of view.

3 Then (and you may find this much more difficult) make a list of any arguments you can think of against the point of view that you have just taken.

Exercise 7

The last exercise has probably shown you that you have many ideas about capital punishment. But you have not done any research yet so your ideas are probably based on opinion rather than on scientific evidence. Now make a list of some facts that you would like to have an answer to in order to make a more informed decision.

Exercise 8

Below you will see some first thoughts of a student who was asked to write an essay on the subject of 'The influence of television on young people'. These notes were made before he did any research into the subject. (The student used the branching method of making notes – see unit 3).

The influence of television on young people

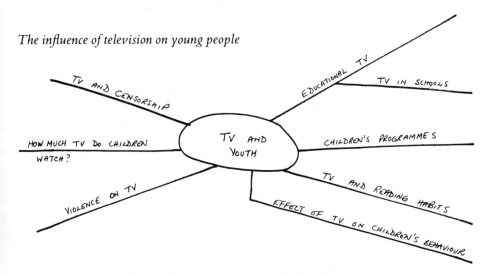

Now try this for yourself. Using any method of making notes that suits you, jot down your first thoughts on *five* of the following topics:

1 The teaching of history in schools.
2 Television and juvenile delinquency.
3 Long-term weather prediction.
4 The usefulness of aid to developing countries.

5 The position of the teacher in society.
6 Public law and private morality.
7 The problem of an expanding world population.
8 Women's liberation.
9 The United Nations and world peace.
10 Equality of wealth in society – is it possible and is it desirable?

TAKE NOTES USING CARDS

Source cards

Your own ideas will only take you so far. You will quickly come to the point where you will have to do some research. How do you get the information you need and how do you record it? We are going to take the second part of the question first because you will need to be properly equipped to do your work of research.

First of all you must note all the sources that you use (i.e. the books and articles that you have referred to for the essay). You may only have a few references on a list made up for you by your tutor. If these are the only sources that you are going to use, then that list is all that you need. But usually in your reading you will come across other books and articles on the same topic.

As far as possible, all the sources that you have used should be recorded on *cards*. Cards are better than a list of titles on a sheet of paper. It is much easier to keep cards in a particular order (alphabetical order of authors, for example) than to keep changing a list on a sheet of paper.

Also, the list of cards can be added to as your reading in the subject increases. If they are kept safe they can be a permanent source of reference to you of books and articles that you have read.

The size of card normally used for this purpose is $5'' \times 3''$ ($127\,\text{mm} \times 76\,\text{mm}$). Below are some examples of the sort of information source cards should contain.

a) *Source card for a book.* You must record the author, title, publisher and date of publication. It is also useful to record the city where the book was published. This is because the publisher may not be a well-known one, or there may be both British and American editions etc. You may also find it useful to put some kind of subject heading for filing the cards away later.

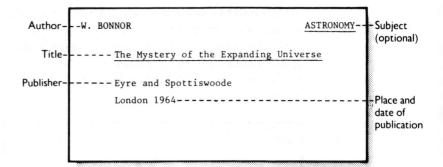

```
Author──┬─-W. BONNOR                            ASTRONOMY──┬─Subject
        │                                                  │ (optional)
Title───┼─────── The Mystery of the Expanding Universe     │
        │                                                  │
Publisher┼────── Eyre and Spottiswoode                     │
        │        London 1964──────────────────────────────┼─Place and
                                                             date of
                                                             publication
```

b) *Source card for a journal article.* Here you must have all the details which enable the article to be found quickly and accurately: full title of the journal, volume number, issue number, date and page reference. (By *issue* we mean the copy of a journal which comes out on a particular date. Issues are collected into *volumes*: usually there is a separate volume for each year.) Notice that the title of the articles is put in single quotes, but the title of the journal is underlined (if printed, it is in *italics*).

```
Author───┬─-Patricia A. DENHAM            LANGUAGE TESTING─┬─Subject
         │                                                 │ (optional)
Title────┼─-'Tests of aural/oral control of language'      │
         │                                                  │
Journal──┼─-·Papua New Guinea Journal of Education          │ Date
Volume no┼─-·Vol. 16 no.3 (1969)──────────────────────────┼─ of volume
Issue no.┼──────────┘                                       │ or issue
         │                                                   │
           pp.11-16─────────────────────────────────────────┼─Page
                                                              reference
```

With magazines that appear weekly and with newspapers it is customary to give the exact date rather than the issue number.

```
Author────┬─-Hugh SIDEY
          │
Title─────┼─-'The presidency:  how much do we want to know?'
          │
Newspaper─┼─-Time
          │
Date──────┼─-3 May 1976
          │
Page──────┼─-p.36
reference
```

c) *Source card for an article or chapter in a book.* Be careful to distinguish between the *author* and the *editor* of a book. Show the difference by putting 'ed.' after the editor's name. Note again that the name of an individual article is usually put in single quotes but the title of the book is underlined or printed in italics.

```
Author-    -D.H.  JONES                    AFRICAN HISTORY- -Subject
                                                             (optional)
Title of-  -'Peoples and kingdoms of the Central Sudan'
article or
chapter
Editor-    -in Roland OLIVER (ed.)
Title of
book .     -The Dawn of African History
Publisher- -Oxford University Press                         Place
                                                            and date
           London 1961- - - - - - - - - - - - - - - - - - - -of publication
```

d) *Other sources.* Sources are not limited to books and periodicals. There are also, for example, university theses or dissertations written by students.

```
Author-       -John Robert LOUDON

Thesis title- -'Mass transfer between gas bubbles and liquids'

Type of thesis- -Ph.D Thesis

University -  -Edinburgh 1968

Date of
presentation- - - - - - - - - - -
```

Whatever your source is, the golden rule is always to give all the information which someone else would need in order to find it again.

Exercise 9

For this and the next two exercises you will need at least three 5″ × 3″ (127 mm × 76 mm) source cards. (If you don't have cards, pieces of paper roughly that size will do.)

Look at the two pages from a book opposite. On the right-hand side is the *title page*. You will notice that some of the information that you need for your source card is missing. This very often happens. On the left-hand side, underneath is the *imprints page* which follows the title page. The missing information can be found on this page. You should be able to write out a source card using the two pages.

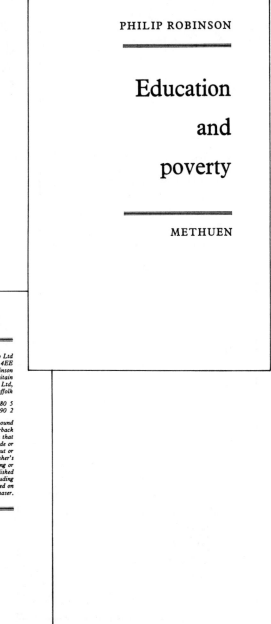

PHILIP ROBINSON

Education
and
poverty

METHUEN

First published in 1976 by Methuen & Co Ltd
11 New Fetter Lane, London EC4P 4EE
© 1976 Philip Robinson
Printed in Great Britain
by Richard Clay (The Chaucer Press), Ltd,
Bungay, Suffolk

ISBN (hardbound) 0 416 55780 5
ISBN (paperback) 0 416 55790 2

Exercise 10

Look at these pages and write out a source card for the book.

Information
in Business and
Administrative
Systems

Ronald Stamper

B. T. Batsford
London

First published 1973
Copyright © Ronald Stamper 1973
Made and printed by
C. Tinling & Co. Ltd
London and Prescot
for the publishers,
B. T. Batsford Ltd
4 Fitzhardinge Street
London W1H 0AH

0 7134 0909 6

Exercise 11

Look at the pages below and write out a source card for the book. (If you are puzzled about what date to put remember that *reprints* are almost always ignored, but that it is usual to take the date of the latest *edition*, noting on your source card which date it is. Or else you can put the date when it was first published and note that information. For more about reprints and editions, look back to unit 2.)

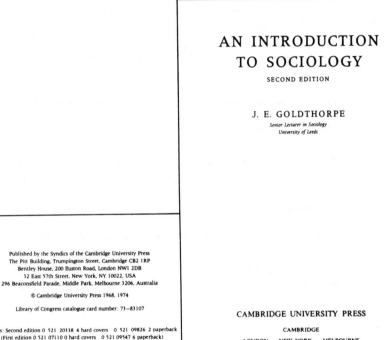

AN INTRODUCTION
TO SOCIOLOGY

SECOND EDITION

J. E. GOLDTHORPE

Senior Lecturer in Sociology
University of Leeds

Published by the Syndics of the Cambridge University Press
The Pitt Building, Trumpington Street, Cambridge CB2 1RP
Bentley House, 200 Euston Road, London NW1 2DB
32 East 57th Street, New York, NY 10022, USA
296 Beaconsfield Parade, Middle Park, Melbourne 3206, Australia

© Cambridge University Press 1968, 1974

Library of Congress catalogue card number: 73–83107

ISBNs: Second edition 0 521 20338 4 hard covers   0 521 09826 2 paperback
(First edition 0 521 07110 0 hard covers   0 521 09547 6 paperback)

First published 1968
Reprinted 1969 1971
Second edition 1974
Reprinted 1975 1976 1978

Photoset and printed in
Malta by Interprint (Malta) Ltd

CAMBRIDGE UNIVERSITY PRESS

CAMBRIDGE

LONDON · NEW YORK · MELBOURNE

Annotated sources. Sometimes it is a good idea to put down a brief summary of an article or book to remind yourself of what it was about. Below is an example of an annotated source. Do not make the notes any longer than you have to; they can of course go on the reverse side of the card.

```
Sydney SAKO                          LANGUAGE TESTING
'Writing proficiency and achievement tests'

TESOL Quarterly
Vol.3 no.3 (1969)

pp. 237-49

(Gives examples of tests covering nine different
areas of language skills, including speech
production.)
```

Annotated source card (article)

The next two exercises will give you some practice in making out source cards. You will need six 5″ × 3″ (127 mm × 76 mm) cards.

Exercise 12

Take any three books that you have in your possession or that you can obtain from a library. (You can start with this one you are reading now!) Write out annotated source cards for the three books you have chosen. Remember to keep your notes brief.

Exercise 13

Now do the same for three articles. You should take two articles from journals related to your subject if any are available – or from any periodical or magazine. Take the third article from a book which is a collection of articles.

Note cards

The next stage is recording notes from the sources. How is this best done?

Once again, the best method is to use cards for recording quotations and notes taken from a lot of books and articles. This is because you will probably want to rearrange the notes when you come to writing your essay, and it is usually easier to do this with cards. It is better to use larger cards for this, because some quotations may be fairly lengthy. (Of course, it is always possible to clip cards together.) Many researchers use $6'' \times 4''$ (152 mm $\times$ 102 mm) cards for this purpose. Note cards can be used for

a) direct quotation from a source
b) your comment on the source
c) your interpretation of what the author says
d) a summary of the author's views.

Always be very clear about what is the author's and what is your own. *The most serious sin in research is to take someone else's ideas (or, worse still, his very words) without acknowledging them.* The chances are that your tutor will be familiar with the texts you have read and will take a very serious view of it if he thinks that you are passing off other people's ideas as your own.

Here are examples of note cards:

Quotation marks to indicate direct quotation

Dots to indicate something omitted

```
            LANGUAGE:   CORRECT USAGE----------  Heading
                                                 (optional)
-----'Even though the language changes century by
century,.. we ought to be able to see that it is
still an important question for every generation
whether it should say this or that, whether this
or that form is correct and so on, and it would be
regrettable if those who were most competent to
decide such questions were to leave the decision
to the less competent.'
                                                 Author,
                                                 date of book,
            Jesperson, 1946, pp. 98-9----        page
                                                 reference
```

Note card with direct quotation

Abbreviation for author's name

```
            LANGUAGE:   CORRECT USAGE----------  Heading
                                                 (optional)
----- J. admits that nothing can stop language from
changing, but insists that 'linguistic historians'
still have a duty to guide the less well-informed--  Direct
on what is acceptable or not acceptable at a         quotation
particular time.

                                                 Author,
            Jesperson, 1946, pp.98-9-            date of book,
                                                 page
                                                 reference
```

Note card with summary

Exercise 14

Look at the passage below which is from a book about the history of timekeeping (i.e. clocks, watches etc).

As time passed, small improvements were made in watches. Brass replaced iron in the making of wheels and screws. Glass crystal was used to protect the faces.

However, for more than one hundred and fifty years watches were regarded as jewellery rather than timekeepers. Cases were made of rock crystal, silver, agate, and gold. They were shaped like butterflies, shells, insects, crosses, or anything else an ingenious artisan could fashion. Mary, Queen of Scots, even had a watch shaped like a skull. The hinged jaw opened to show the dial.

Then in 1685 a major advance in watchmaking occurred. Robert Hooke, who had invented the anchor escapement for clocks, found that a vibrating spring would provide a regular rhythm for a watch just as a pendulum did for a clock. He made his spring from a hog's bristle, because it was tough enough to coil and uncoil again and again without breaking. For this reason, it was called a hairspring. It has kept this name although bristles have long since been replaced by metal springs.

The hairspring brought increased accuracy to watches. Shortly after its invention, watchmakers began putting minute hands on their timepieces. Until then watches had been so inaccurate, even as to the hour, that it was not uncommon for a man to carry as many as three in order to check one against another. There had been no use at all in bothering with minutes.

(From K. K. Borland and H. S. Speicher: *Clocks, from Shadow to Atom* (World's Work Publishers, Tadworth, Surrey, 1970; pp. 45–7))

1 Make a source card for this book.
2 Find a sentence where the authors give an example of how inaccurate early watches used to be. Make a quotation note card for it.
3 The authors give an unusual example of a decorative watch used by Mary, Queen of Scots. Make out a quotation note card for it.
4 This passage emphasises the importance of the *hairspring* to timekeeping. Make up a summary note card bringing out this point, in two or three sentences.

Exercise 15

Look at the passage below which is from a book about geology.

Today's scientists are making an international effort to learn more about the causes of quakes and to find better methods of prediction and ways to protect people and their property against them. Although they already know something of the causes and they can identify earthquakes by instruments, the exact causes are still being debated. In fact, there are so many new findings, new theories, and new methods of learning about the earth that geology is sometimes thought of as a science in a state of revolution. In the light of new knowledge, old textbooks no longer tell the true story of the earth. And so it is with the study of earthquakes.

One point on which geologists agree is that strong earthquakes are due, mainly, to the fracturing of great masses of rock many miles beneath the earth's surface. Rock masses slip and slide along a plane of fracture, which is called a fault. Great blocks of rock perhaps ten miles wide, may be moved bodily, and displaced as much as fifty feet along the fault. It is easy to see why the earth above trembles, causing catastrophe to large areas.

A *tsunami* is due to a sudden rising or dropping of the ocean floor. You might be travelling in a ship at sea where the water is quite deep when far below you rocks slip and a rift opens in the bed of the ocean. Your ship might be carried ashore by the tremendous wave that results from such an earthquake, but it is more likely that you would be totally unaware of any change at all, because the distance between crests of such waves is often as far apart as one hundred miles.

In some areas where destructive waves roll ashore with unusual frequency, natives race for the hills as soon as strong shocks are felt along the coast.

(From Margaret O. Hyde: *The Earth in Action* (Collins, London, 1969; pp. 50–1))

1 Make out a source card for this book.
2 What does the author say about the present state of geology as a science? Make out a quotation note card for your answer.
3 According to the author, what is the generally-agreed reason for strong earthquakes? Make out a quotation note card for it.
4 Using the information in the passage explain in your own words what a *tsunami* is. Make out a summary card for this information.

Storing references. Now that you are aware of the technique of using note cards, try to get into the habit of using it whenever you read something in a book or journal that relates to your subject. You can use one of the commercially-prepared card boxes available in most stationers' shops for storing the cards. A cheaper alternative is to use an old shoe box with elastic bands to keep the cards together.

As your collection of cards grows, you may want to classify them, arranging them alphabetically by author, or by subject. You can separate cards on different subjects etc by using 'guide cards': these are coloured and slightly larger than the normal ones so that you can put a title on them which can be easily seen. Again, it is easy to make your own guide cards.

Finding a book from the library catalogue

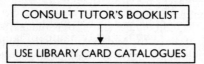

Sometimes your tutor will give you a list of *references* for your essay. These are usually books which your tutor knows are available in the college or university library.

First of all you must find out whether the library actually has the book and, if so, whereabouts in the library it is to be found. To do this you will have to consult the library *catalogue*.

The catalogue may be in the form of large loose-leaf books, but more commonly it takes the form of cards something like the source cards you used for making up your own list of books.

The cards will usually be arranged alphabetically by *author* or by *title* or perhaps by both author and title. (They may also be arranged by subject, but we shall come to that later.) This means that you can usually find a book in the card catalogue if you know either the author or the title.

Exercise 16

The cards will usually be kept in boxes. At the front of each box there will be something to show you which cards that particular box contains. Here is an example of how a particular set of boxes in a library might be arranged:

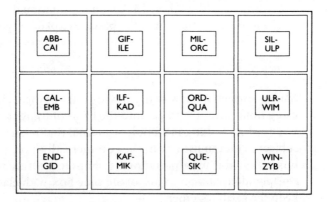

Card catalogue boxes

This particular catalogue is arranged according to authors' names. There is a label at the front of each box of catalogue cards. This label shows the first three letters of the name on the first card, in the box, and the first three letters of the name on the last card. In the first box the first card gives the details of a book by an author named Abbot; the last card gives the details of a book by an author whose name is Cairns. The letters on the outside are, therefore, ABB–CAI. Here is a list of names of famous British authors. In which box would you expect to find reference-cards for them?

1 W. Somerset Maugham
2 Robert Louis Stevenson
3 Alfred Lord Tennyson
4 Evelyn Waugh
5 Graham Greene

6 Geoffrey Chaucer
7 John Keats
8 Robert Browning
9 William Wordsworth
10 Thomas Hardy

Here is an example of a catalogue card (catalogued by author):

```
Author------HERRIOT, Peter
                                                    401.9-    Shelf mark
Title---------Language and Teaching: a psychological view

Publishing-----London:  Methuen, 1971
details
                                                               Contains
Length------·109 p.                       Glossary   Bibl.--  glossary
Accession-----97547                                           Contains
numbers -----97294                                            bibliography
```

You will see that it gives the following information:
1 the name of the author or editor.
2 the *shelf-mark* indicating which section of the library the book is in. (Sometimes this is known as the *call number*.)
3 the title.
4 the publishing details: where it was published, the name of the publisher, the date of publication.
5 the length – number of pages. Sometimes you will see, for example:
   xi, 229p.
   This means that the book has 11 pages of introductory material and 229 pages of main text.
6 other information: whether the book contains a glossary, bibliography etc. Sometimes you are told whether the book has illustrations, maps, diagrams, whether it is part of a series, and so on.
7 accession numbers. Every single copy of a book can be identified by its accession number which it gets when it comes into the library. This is useful as it tells you how many copies are available.

The example given is an author card, so the author's name comes first. With a title card, it would be the title of the book that comes first. Different libraries have different systems and will give you various kinds of information; but all cards should give you the author's name, the title, and the shelf-mark. The name and title help you to identify the book, and the shelf-mark enables you to find it in the library.

Exercice 17

Here is another library catalogue card (catalogued by author):

```
WEBBER, David (ed.)                              530

      Modern Physics : selected readings

      Harmondsworth, Middlesex : Penguin 1971


      319 p.                                  Bibl.
      96230
```

Library reference card (by author)

Use the card to answer these questions:
1 What does the abbreviation 'ed.' stand for?
2 What is the publisher and date of publication?
3 What is the shelf mark?
4 Does the book have a bibliography?
5 How many copies does the library have?

Exercice 18

Here is another library catalogue card (catalogued by author):

```
MILLER, George A.                                150


        Psychology : the science of mental life

      London : Hutchinson 1964
                  (Hutchinson Science Library)

      388 p.    Illus.   Bibl.   Glossary.

      33401          33402          33404
      33405          36982          40696
```

Library reference card (by author)

116

Use the card to answer these questions:

1 Who wrote this book?
2 What is the shelf-mark?
3 When was it published?
4 Is it part of a series?
5 If you wanted to know the meanings of certain psychological terms, is there any particular way this book might be able to help you?
6 How many copies does the library have?

Author and title cards are arranged alphabetically, so that anyone who can use a dictionary can use a library catalogue. But there are some special points for you to watch for:

1 Author cards are arranged in order of the authors' *surnames* (last names) so a book by the writer Thomas Hardy will appear under 'Hardy' and probably be written like this:
   HARDY, Thomas
2 When a library contains more than one book by the same author, the cards are arranged in alphabetical order of the *title*: so, for example, we would have the next two cards in this order:
   DICKENS, Charles: *Great Expectations*
   DICKENS, Charles: *Hard Times*
3 When the two authors have the same surnames, you go by their first names. So 'DICKENS, Charles' will come before 'DICKENS, Monica'.
4 Sometimes you may be doubtful about what the actual surname is. In that case you may have to check up the name more than once. For example, with a name like 'Leonard De Vries' you might check up 'De Vries' first and, if you did not find it there, then you would try under 'Vries'. Often the catalogue will help you by having a card which says:
   DE VRIES, Leonard. See VRIES, Leonard De
   This means that you must check the author's card under the name 'Vries'.
5 Names beginning with Mac-, Mc- M^c- etc are usually filed under Mac-. So, 'Macintyre' will come after 'Mabon' but before 'Madison'. The following names are in the correct order:
   McAdam, McArthur, MacClure, MacInnes, McKee, Macrae, MacRobert.

Exercise 19

Below is a list of authors and their books. Rearrange them in the order you would expect to find them in an author card catalogue. Surnames are printed in block capitals.

1 Louis MADELIN: *The French Revolution*
2 Robert McADAM and David DAVIDSON: *Mine Rescue Work*
3 Salvador de MADARIAGA: *Theory and Practice in International Relations*
4 Harry Alfred MADDOX: *Printing: its history, practice and progress*
5 Thomas Babington MACAULEY: *History of England*
6 Rose MACAULEY: *On Linguistic Changes*

Exercise 20

Finding the *titles* of books in a catalogue is easier. You go by the first word of the title, except that you usually ignore the articles (i.e. *a/an* and *the*). For example, a book called *The Art of Botanical Illustration* will be filed under the letter A (for *Art*) and not T (for *The*). Here is a list of books about clinical medicine. (The list is taken from *British Scientific and Technical Books 1953–57*, edited by L. J. Anthony, and published for ASLIB by James Clarke, Cambridge 1960.) If you wanted to find these titles in a title catalogue, which letter would you check under?

1 A. R. D. Adams and B. G. Maegraith: *Tropical Medicine for Nurses*
2 G. E. Beaumont: *The Clinical Approach in Medical Practice*
3 G. E. Beaumont: *Medicine, Essentials for Practitioners and Students*
4 E. T. Bell: *A Textbook of Pathology*
5 G. P. Wright: *An Introduction to Pathology*

Finding the book on the shelf

We have said before that every book has a shelf-mark or call number which enables you to find it. This shelf-mark will be taken from some system of classification. Different libraries have different systems of classification, but one very popular system is called the *Dewey Decimal Classification*.

The idea of this system is that books in the same subject area will be grouped together. See the table below on the Dewey Decimal Classification. You do not have to memorise the system, of course, but it may be useful for you to know which main classes contain subjects that are of special interest to you.

The Dewey Decimal Classification

The Dewey Decimal Classification is divided into ten main classes, as follows:

000–099	General works (including libraries, journalism, general encyclopedias etc)
100–199	Philosophy and Psychology
200–299	Religion
300–399	Social Sciences
400–499	Language
500–599	Science
600–699	Applied Science and Useful Arts
700–799	Fine Arts and Recreation
800–899	Literature
900–999	History, Geography

Each of these classes may be divided into ten smaller classes. Let us take Science, for example (500–599). We have:

500		Science in General
	510	Mathematics
	520	Astronomy
	530	Physics
	540	Chemistry
	550	Geology
	560	Fossils
	570	Biology
	580	Botany
	590	Zoology

Each of these classes may be further divided, for example:

500			Science in General
	590		Zoology in General
		591	Animals – habits and behaviour
		592	Invertebrates – animals without backbones
		593	Sponges, corals, jellyfish etc
		594	Molluscs – snails, shell-fish, sea-shells
		595	Other invertebrates – worms, crabs, spiders etc.
		596	Vertebrates – sea squirts and sea grapes
		597	Fishes
		598	Reptiles and birds
		599	Mammals

Doing the next exercise should help you to familiarise yourself with this system. Remember that the other systems you are likely to come across will be based on similar principles.

Exercise 21

Below is a list of references on different subjects. Which of the ten main classes would you expect to find each book classified under? Write down the class number, e.g. 200–299, 700–799 etc. (It may help you to know that each of the ten main classes is represented by a title!)

1 W. Montgomery Watt: *The Majesty that was Islam: the Islamic World 661–1100* (Sidgwick and Jackson 1974)
2 H. W. Fowler: *A Dictionary of Modern English Usage* second edition (Oxford University Press 1964)
3 Alan Jeffreys (ed.): *The Art of the Librarian* (Oriel Press 1973)
4 A. C. Bouquet: *Sacred Books of the World* (Cassell 1962)
5 Tony Richardson and Nikos Stangos: *Concepts of Modern Art* (Pelican Books 1974)
6 Adam Smith: *Powers of Mind* (Random House 1975)
7 T. E. Smith (ed.): *Politics of Family Planning in the Third World* (Allen & Unwin 1973)
8 Bruce Withers and Stanley Vipond: *Irrigation Design and Practice* (Batsford 1974)
9 J. W. Binns: *Latin Literature of the Fourth Century* (Routledge 1974)
10 W. Cochrane: *The Dynamics of Atoms in Crystals* (Edward Arnold 1973)

Do not worry if you found some of the books difficult to classify: after all, classifying books is a librarian's job – you have only to find them! Nevertheless, if you had to think carefully about some of the classifications, you will understand more easily why a particular book you are looking for may not be where you expect to find it. If you cannot find a book on the shelf that you would expect, always check back to the author or title catalogue. It may have been classified for some good reason under another class number, and therefore be found elsewhere in the library.

We have been talking so far about books. Some of the references you are given may be for periodicals, i.e. journals, magazines etc. This should not be too difficult. Libraries usually have a *periodicals index* which lists all the periodicals which the library takes. It will also indicate *how long* the library has been taking a particular periodical, e.g. since 1964, or since 1952.

IF NECESSARY,
USE
INTER-LIBRARY
LOAN

Supposing that the book or article is not available in the library? Many libraries have what are called *inter-library loan* facilities with other libraries. This means that the librarian can order the book for you from another library if you give him all the details.

In the same way you can sometimes get photo-copies of articles from periodicals which your own college or university library does not hold.

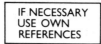

IF NECESSARY
USE OWN
REFERENCES

You may want to study some other books on the subject, apart from the ones on your tutor's list. The first thing to do is to check whether the books you have been recommended contain any bibliographies or recommended reading. Check them to see if there is anything suitable. Then you could ask your tutor for further suggestions.

Finding your own references

So far we have been dealing with the fairly straightforward matter of locating books and articles which have been recommended. Tutors usually recommend only books or articles which they know are easily available.

But what if you have no references? You may be doing some research on your own, or you may want to read about some subject just as a matter of interest.

We have already mentioned asking your tutor for information or using the bibliographies of text books that you have already used. Now we shall go on to look at the way in which you can use the facilities of your college or university library. Look at programme 2 on p. 99 above. We have already discussed the first four steps of the programme, and we go on to:

USE
LIBRARY
FACILITIES

Any time you can spare for finding out about your college or university library will be time well spent. Some students spend two or three years of study at a university without being fully aware of all the help that they can get from the library. There will probably be some guide to the library's services. Read it carefully. Do not be afraid to ask the library staff for information and advice.

> GENERAL
> ENCYCLOPEDIAS

When you want to find out something about a subject, especially a subject which is new to you, a good place to start might be a *general encyclopedia* (often spelled *encyclopaedia*). General encyclopedias are intended for the non-specialist, but they cover most areas of human knowledge. Here are some of the best known general encyclopedias:
Encyclopaedia Britannica
Chambers Encyclopaedia
Everymans Encyclopaedia
Colliers Encyclopedia
The New Columbia Encyclopedia
The World Book Encyclopedia

All these encyclopedias have bibliographies at the end of each article, except the *Colliers Encyclopedia*, which has a bibliography along with the index in a separate volume. Although these encyclopedias are all very large, they are fairly simple to use. The topics are arranged alphabetically as in a dictionary. Each one also has a good index to help you to get the information you need.

Exercise 22

Opposite you will find a page from the 1978 edition of *The World Book Encyclopedia*. The volumes are numbered according to the letter with which the entries in that particular volume begin. Thus all the entries beginning with T will appear in the T volume. A few letters (e.g. C) are divided between two volumes (e.g. C and Ci). The numbers following the letter refer to the page, so T: 276 refers to p. 276 in the T volume. A feature of this encyclopedia is the special sections on certain topics: the pages in these sections have letters as well as numbers: e.g. 154a, 154b etc.

Where in *The World Book Encyclopedia* you would find information on:
1 The Nurek Dam in the Vaksh River in Russia
2 Nutritional diseases (i.e. diseases related to food and diet)

(From *The World Book Encyclopedia*, vol. 22)

3 A picture of Nylon fibre (US spelling: fiber)
4 Red Cross Nursing and Health Programmes (US spelling: programs)
5 The place of nymphs in Greek mythology
6 A photograph of President Nyerere of Tanzania
7 The famous Finnish athlete Paavo Nurmi
8 The importance of vitamins in diet

SPECIALISED
REFERENCE BOOKS

You may find the information you want in a specialised reference book. Most subjects have their own dictionaries and encyclopedias: examples are *Chambers Dictionary of Science and Technology* (edited by T. C. Collocott and A. B. Dobson, Chambers 1974); *Dictionary of Management* (edited by D. French and H. Saward, Gower Press, Epping 1975).

Exercise 23

Make a list of the specialised reference books which your library has for your subject. Divide the list into 1 dictionaries, 2 encyclopedias, 3 other works of reference. (You may not be able to find titles for all three headings, but there should be something under 1 or 2.)

There are also, of course, other specialised reference books where you can get precise information on a huge variety of subjects.

Here are some examples:
1 English dictionaries
2 Bilingual dictionaries (e.g. English–French, Swahili–English)
3 Dictionaries of abbreviations
4 Gazetteers (giving place names) and atlases
5 Thesauruses (which give words grouped together by their meaning: the most famous is *Roget's Thesaurus*)
6 Biographical dictionaries (the most famous one is *Who's Who* which gives details of the lives of famous people still living)
7 Dictionaries of quotations
8 Dudens (These useful books have drawings of a huge variety of objects, and give the names of the objects and their parts. They exist for several languages e.g. *The English Duden.*)
9 Reference grammars and guides to correct usage
10 Yearbooks, i.e. books which appear every year giving up-to-date information. For example, for higher education alone, there are:

World of Learning (Europa Publications)
Barron's Profiles of American Colleges (Barron's Educational Services, New York)
Which University? (Haymarket Publishers)
Higher Education in the United Kingdom (Longman, for The British Council and The Association of Commonwealth Universities).

This list could be made much longer. The point to remember is that if there is any kind of general or specialised information that you need, a good library will help you to find it.

Exercise 24

What kind of specialised reference book would help you to find the following information (you do not have to supply the information – yet!):

1 What are the rules for forming the plurals of 'foreign' words in English, such as *bacillus* and *formula*?
2 What do the initials WHO stand for?
3 What is the population of Montreal?
4 Ben Nevis is the highest mountain in Britain. Is it close to Glasgow?
5 Which British Universities offer courses on . . . . . .? (Insert any subject that you are interested in.)
6 When was the Emperor Napoleon born?
7 Who said: 'The reports of my death are greatly exaggerated'?
8 What is the meaning of the idiom *To keep one's shirt on*?
9 What is another word one could use instead of *spectator* (i.e. a synonym for *spectator*)?
10 Where could one find a drawing of the main parts of a motor car with the English names for them?

Exercise 25

If you do not know the answers to any of the questions in exercise 24 – find them out!

> SUBJECT
> INDEXES

Another way of getting further references is to see what your library has available in the way of books on a particular topic. You can do this by browsing around the shelves where books on your subject are kept – and you may be lucky. On the other hand, a book that could be useful to you may have been borrowed by someone else. Or perhaps a relevant book may be located somewhere else in the library.

Instead of going straight to the shelves, you can check whether the library has a *subject index*. The following extract shows what a subject index looks like:

Subject heading	Class no.
New Towns: Great Britain	711.40942
New Towns: Social Planning	309.26
New York: Geography	917.471
New Zealand: Education	370.9931
New Zealand: Elementary Education	372.9931
New Zealand: Geography	919.31
New Zealand: History	993.1
New Zealand: Maps	912.931
New Zealand: Travel	919.31
Newcomen, Thomas: Steam Engineering	621.1
Newfoundland: Geography	917.18
Newland, John: Education: Scotland	370.941
Newlyn: Geography	914.237
Newman, John Henry (Cardinal): Criticism	824.8
Newspapers	070.
Newspapers: First World War	940.3
Newspapers: Periodicals	070.48
Newspapers: Photography	778.9907
Newton, Sir Isaac: Biography	509.
Ngoni: Malawi: Anthropology	572.96897
Nicene Creed	238.14
Nicholson, Ben: Painting	759.2
Nicholson, Reynold: Biography	942.08
Nickel: Manufactures	673.733
Nickel: Refining	622.348
Nicolson, Harold: Biography	942.082
Niebuhr, Reinhold: Christian Theology	230.
Nietzsche, Friedrich Wilhelm: Philosophy: Criticism	193.9
Niger River: Exploration	916.62
Nigeria: Agriculture	630.09669
Nigeria: Anthropology	572.9669
Nigeria: Economics	330.9669
Nigeria: Education	370.9669
Nigeria: Geography	916.69
Nigeria: Hill Farmers: Communities	301.35
Nigeria: History	966.9
Nigeria: Language	496.3
Nigeria: Travel	916.69
Nightingale, Florence: Biography	942.08
Nightmares: Psychology	154.63

The subjects are listed on the left-hand side and the class number on the right. This library also has a classified card catalogue which lists all the books in the library in order of their Dewey Decimal Number. For example, if you want to find out about the History of Nigeria you would check the classified catalogue under 966.9. There you would find all the cards connected with the books that the library has on Nigerian History. You can then go through the cards to see whether any of the titles look promising.

In doing the next exercise you will notice an important point: in checking the subject index you may not always find out what you want under the first heading that you check. You may have to check under a *more general* heading or a *more specific (precise)* heading. For example, if you check up *badminton* and find nothing you could try under *sports* or *indoor sports*.

Exercise 26

The purpose of this exercise is to make you familiar with how the subject index works. Write down the class number under which you would expect to find the information you need for dealing with each topic. All the answers can be found by referring to the extract above.

1 You are writing a paper on secondary schools in Nigeria and you need some source material.
2 You are a student in Modern Urban Studies and you are interested in the development of new towns in Great Britain.
3 You know that Yoruba is a language spoken in Nigeria and you want to find out more about it.
4 You are studying metallurgy and interested in finding out how different metals are refined.
5 You are studying the psychology of sleep.

BIBLIOGRAPHIES

Now we come to a very important source of information – bibliographies, which may be published as separate books. Bibliographies are simply lists of books etc. They may be classified lists i.e. books etc listed under various headings, or they may be annotated with comments on the books etc to help you decide whether they will be of use or interest to you.

SUBJECT
BIBLIOGRAPHIES

The most useful kind of bibliography will be one on your own subject (e.g. Engineering, Literature, Building, Science, etc). You can be sure that every major subject has had a bibliography published for it, and most subjects have annual bibliographies which keep up-to-date with the latest books. You will usually find subject bibliographies by checking under the class number. In the Dewey Decimal Classification, for example, bibliographies for the Social Sciences will be classified under 300–399.

Exercise 27

Find out from the library if it has any bibliographies for your subject. If it does have any, make a note of them.

```
GENERAL
BIBLIOGRAPHIES
```

In addition to the subject bibliographies, there are also general bibliographies, which list all the books which appear every year. One example is *The Cumulative Book Index* published by the H. H. Wilson Company of New York. Another example is *The British National Bibliography (BNB)*. The entries in the *BNB* are organised according to the Dewey Decimal classification, but it also has an author and title index. Here is a sample entry:

339.2 — Income. Distribution. Measurement.
Lectures, speeches
Sen, Amartya Kumar. On economic inequality:
the Radcliffe lectures, delivered in the
University of Warwick, 1972 / [by] Amartya
Sen. — Oxford : Clarendon Press, 1973. — xi,
118p : ill ; 21 cm. — (Radcliffe lectures)
Bibl.: p.107-113. — Index.
ISBN 0-19-828182-x : £2.10.
ISBN 0-19-828193-5 Pbk: £0.90.

(B74-00738)

(Note: the ISBN number is a publisher's number to be used when ordering a particular book).

Exercise 28

Use the sample entry above to answer these questions.
1   What is the short title of the book (three words)?
2   What is the subject matter of the book?
3   What is the author's name?
4   When was it published?
5   Where was it published?
6   What is the name of the publisher?
7   Does it have any illustrations?
8   Does it have a bibliography?
9   Does it have an index?

10 How many pages does it have?

11 How much does the hardback cost?

12 How much does the paperback edition cost?

You can see that even the short entries in the *BNB* give you a lot of information, especially about publication details. Unfortunately, there are not so many details about the content of the book itself. For this you need an *annotated* bibliography. There are two well-known annotated bibliographies which appear regularly: the *British Book News*, which gives brief notes on each book listed, and *Book Review Digest* (American) which usually gives at least two reviews of each book, so that you do not have to rely on the verdict of one critic.

Exercise 29

Look at the annotation from *British Book News* on the book called *Mars* by Patrick Moore and Charles A. Cross. Answer the questions that follow.

ASTRONOMY

Mars Patrick Moore, Charles A. Cross *Mitchell Beazley* £4·85 1973 34 cm 48 pages Maps Illustrations Index SBN 85533 012 0

This 'first complete atlas of Mars and its moons' brings the results of spacecraft exploration of the planet into the reach of everyone. The book begins by identifying Mars among the planets of the Solar System. It tells of the global properties; of the visual and photographic observations made with Earth-based telescopes; the main surface features and the changes of the Martian atmosphere. The text and presentation of this material is adequate but not without imperfections. The importance of this book, and the reason why it should be on the shelves of every library, lies in the Mariner spacecraft photography, the charts of the entire surface drawn to a uniform scale of 1: 23,500,000, and the succinct introduction to Martian topography. Although there will undoubtedly be better atlases in the future, this one is likely to lead the field for several years.

(523·43)

1 Why are the words 'first complete atlas of Mars and its moons' in quotation marks?

2 Give *one* reason why, according to the reviewer, this book is an important one.

3 Does the reviewer think that the book will soon be out-of-date?

Revision

Exercise 30

Look at programmes 1 and 2 again.
1 Check through the squares that you marked (?). Do you know
   what they signify now? If you do, mark them with a ✓
   (procedure used by you) or an X (procedure not used by you).
2 Now look at the ones you marked X at the beginning. Do you
   agree with that marking?

Unit 6   Writing an essay   ii) Organisation

In unit 5, we discussed some of the things involved in researching an essay. In this unit we shall be discussing various aspects of the organisation of your material. It is worth noting that most of the comments in this unit apply equally well to answering examination questions.

Organisation of your material will often depend on what kind of essay you have to write. Here are some of the kinds of activities you may become involved with when writing an essay. Note that two or more of these activities may be involved in the same piece of work.

1 Telling how one thing happened after another.   (*Narrative*)
2 Comparing and contrasting.   (*Comparison*)
3 Describing the appearance of something.   (*Static description*)
4 Describing how something works, is done etc.   (*Process description*)
5 Explaining how one thing causes another.   (*Cause and effect*)
6 Putting forward arguments, evidence etc.   (*Discussion*)
7 Explaining what a term means.   (*Definition*)
8 Illustrating a topic with examples, analogy etc.   (*Illustration*)
(For further information, see the glossary at the end of this unit, pp. 154–5.)

Exercise 1

Below is a list of essay titles which students have been asked to write. Which activity or activities, as listed above, do you think the title for each essay requires?

1 (Biology) How would you set up an aquarium and a vivarium?
2 (Sociology) Examine the view that the functions of the family in industrial societies have been taken over by other agencies.
3 (Literature) Compare and contrast Ibsen's and Chekhov's views on art as reflected in at least *one* play by each writer.
4 (Linguistics) Explain briefly what is meant by 'descriptive grammar' and 'intuitive grammar'.
5 (Economics) To what extent were the industrial ills of the 1920s a product of World War I?

6 (History) How far was the Jacobite rebellion of 1745 simply a repeat performance of the 1715 rebellion?

7 (History) Trace in outline the development of the British Labour Party as a political force between 1918 and 1929.

8 (Biology) Give an account of the techniques you would use to isolate, type and quantify the coliform flora of a water source.

9 (Classical Studies) Describe the layout of a typical Roman military camp.

10 (Geography) Mention some ways in which the development of industry can be affected by environmental factors. Illustrate your answer by referring where possible to the Geography of England.

D-words

The title of an essay can usually be divided into two parts:

1 There are the words or phrases which direct you as to what you have to do. We can call these 'D-words' (for 'direction words').

2 There are the words or phrases which relate the subject of the essay. We can call these 'content words'.

For example, in the first two essays listed in exercise 1, the D-words are *How* and *Examine the view (that)*. Sometimes certain D-words go with a certain kind of activity, e.g. *compare* and *contrast* usually indicate a comparison activity.

Exercise 2

Copy down or underline the D-words in exercise 1, numbers 3 to 10. Make a note of which D-words go with which activities in these examples.

Exercise 3

Go over any examination papers or lists of essays that you have available. (Copies of past examination papers are sometimes kept in college or university libraries.) List any D-words which occur in the essay titles; put beside each D-word the type of activity which that particular title requires.

Listing

There are some techniques which are used in practically every essay. One of these is the technique of *listing* the ideas that you are going to use in the essay. This has to be done before anything else.

Lists can be *ordered* or *random*. Random lists are very useful if you want to get down some ideas on paper before you forget them. Before you start writing your essay, however, the lists should be *ordered*, so that you can make sense of them. There are various methods of ordering points, including:

a) by order of importance (most important point coming first or last)
b) by categories (things which have something in common grouped together)
c) by order in time (narrative).

Exercise 4

Below is a random list taken from some articles about music. Make the list more ordered. What method or methods are you going to use? (To help you, some background information has been given.)

Opera	(play with music in which most or all of the words are sung)
Piano	(keyboard instrument, played by pressing down the keys with the fingers)
Mozart	(Austrian composer, 1756–91)
Liszt	(Hungarian composer, 1811–86)
Ballet	(sort of play without words performed to music by dancers)
Violin	(stringed instrument, played with a bow)
Symphony	(musical composition played by an orchestra)
Beethoven	(German composer, 1770–1827)
Chopin	(Polish composer, 1810–49)
Sonata	(musical composition, usually for one or two instruments)
Guitar	(stringed instrument, played by plucking with the fingers)

Exercise 5

Choose one (or more) of the following topics. Think about the topic and jot down a list of the main items you would like to mention. Then, organise your ideas according to some kind of classification. Lastly, write one or two paragraphs on the topic.

Methods of buying and selling	Housing
Means of transport	The animal kingdom
Sports and pastimes	Useful inventions
Climate and weather conditions	Trades and professions
Military organisation	Traditional art

Exercise 6

Imagine that you have been asked to give a brief talk (4–5 minutes, i.e. about 400–500 words) to a class of schoolchildren on your native country, or some aspect of it, e.g. way of life, geography etc. First, make a list of points as they occur to you. Then, make them into an ordered list. Lastly, write out your talk.

Vocabulary guide: listing

group	include
set	comprise (often, be comprised
class	of . . .)
kind	contain
variety	take in
division	be numbered among
subdivision	be included in
(also subgroup, subset)	be grouped with
exclude	excluding
except	excepting
	except for
	with the exception of
first, second, third . . .	also
firstly, secondly, thirdly . . .	in addition
finally	likewise
lastly	similarly
	in the same way

Narrative

One very common type of organisation is where we simply tell what happened. This is the method we use when telling a story, and it is called *narrative*. The simplest kind of narrative is the one which follows *chronological order*, i.e. which tells the events in the order in which they occurred. Is the following in strict chronological order – or not?

'I went to the English class at 11. Before that I had a coffee with Stephen. I needed a coffee – I didn't have anything for breakfast! After the class, I went off and ate a hearty lunch.'

Unless you have a good reason for not doing so, it is best to follow chronological order.

Exercise 7

A student was asked to write an essay on 'How the Braille system was invented'. (The Braille system is a method by which the blind can read by feeling raised dots on a page.) Here are some of his notes – but they are a bit jumbled, and you must indicate the *chronological order*.

a) Braille was accidentally blinded when he was 3 years old.
b) Louis Braille was born in France in 1809.
c) At the age of ten, he was sent to a special school for the blind.
d) In his early twenties, he was successful and invented the Braille system, which is still in use today.
e) He did not think much of the methods of teaching the blind which were used at the special school.
f) Braille decided to see if he could invent a system similar to night-writing to enable the blind to read.
g) He met a Captain Barbier who told him about a night-writing system which soldiers could use to read in the dark.

Exercise 8

It often happens that other materials have to be blended (mixed) with narrative. The previous notes, for example, tell us about the life of Braille. They do not tell us much about the *Braille system*, which is the topic of the essay. Here are some more notes which are relevant. Using these notes, and the previous ones, write an essay on 'How the Braille system was invented'.

Method used when Braille was at the special school:
large letters made out of cloth
each letter about 3 inches high
children's fingers guided over the shapes of the letters.

Night-writing system:
made by a shoemaker's tool pushed into cardboard holes in the shape of dots and dashes
a certain arrangement of dots and dashes gave a command
soldiers could 'read' the command at night-time without using a light.

Braille system:
uses only dots
(people's fingers are more sensitive to dots than dashes)
dots can be arranged in 63 different ways
this covers all the letters of the alphabet, punctuation, and even some common words.

Vocabulary guide: narrative (see also guide: listing, p. 134)

then	before this/that
next	prior to
subsequently	formerly
afterwards	
finally	while
eventually	at the same time
simultaneously	at last
in the end	meanwhile

Exercise 9

'The story of my education'. Write a short account (about a page or so) of the stages of your education, mentioning (perhaps) the main things which you think you learnt at each stage.

Comparison

When we *compare* things we look for ways in which they are the same, or perhaps similar; when we *contrast* things, we look for ways in which they are dissimilar or different.

There are basically two ways in which we can write essays that involve comparison and/or contrast. One way is to write down all the main points about one of the subjects to be compared, and then to take all the main points about the other subject, like this:

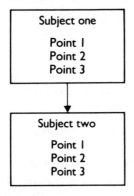

The other way is to take each point in turn and to contrast them immediately, like this:

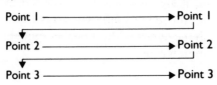

136

The first method is sometimes better for short, simple topics; the second method may be better for longer, more complex topics.

Exercise 10

Imagine that you have been asked to write an essay comparing the British and American systems of government. You have checked up some reference books and come up with the facts listed below. You are now about to write your essay.
1. Decide how you are going to arrange the material and make some outline notes.
2. Write one or two paragraphs comparing the British and American systems of government.

United Kingdom
1. Parliament consists of House of Lords and House of Commons.
2. House of Commons is elected at least every 5 years, sometimes less.
3. The Queen is the Head of State. By tradition, she does not interfere in politics.
4. The House of Lords is not elected.
5. No written constitution.
6. Judges cannot make constitutional decisions.
7. The political leader of the country is the Prime Minister, who is usually also the leader of the largest party in the House of Commons.

U.S.A.
1. The President is both the political leader and the Head of State.
2. The President is *not* a member of Congress.
3. Congress can refuse to pass bills suggested by the President.
4. The President can veto bills which Congress passes.
5. Congress consists of the Senate and the House of Representatives.
6. The Senate consists of 2 senators from every state: one third of the senators are elected every 6 years.
7. The House of Representatives is elected every two years.
8. The Supreme Court (9 judges) interprets the written constitution.

constitutional decisions: decisions about the political organisation of the country.
veto: refuse to put into effect.

Exercise 11

Write a few paragraphs on one or more of the following topics. Do the work in two stages. First, make a two-column list as you saw in the previous exercise and put it into order. Then write the paragraphs.

1 The British *or* American system of government and that of your own country
2 The organisation of social life in Britain and in your own country
3 Any two sports or hobbies that you are familiar with
4 The social roles of men and women in your society (e.g. the jobs that men and women are expected to do, the ways in which they are expected to behave etc)
5 Your chosen career or profession and any other career/ profession that you know about.

Vocabulary guide: comparison

(points of) similarity	resemble
resemblance	appear/seem like
correspondence	put one in mind of
	correspond to
close/marked resemblance	
similar	compare (with/to)
not unlike	liken (to)
the same	make a comparison (with)
identical	
connected with	similarly
resembling	correspondingly
	in the same way
	likewise
difference	differ from
distinction	distinguish
different from	make a distinction between
dissimilar	bear no resemblance to
unlike	
opposed	
on the contrary	
conversely	
in contrast	
on the other hand	

Static description

Very often we have to describe the appearance or layout of something. We shall refer to this as static description. The main things about static description are that

1 it should be *orderly*. You should have some organisation in your description, e.g. general to particular, more important to less important, front to back, etc.
2 it should be *clear*. The reader should have a clear picture in his mind of what you are describing.
3 it should be *accurate*. The details must be correct.
4 it should be *complete*. Nothing important should be missed out.

It is often better to start with the general appearance or main aspects of what you are describing and then go on to details. The exercises which follow should give you a chance to test your descriptive powers in a not-too-serious way.

Exercise 12

Pick one of the shapes below. Write as accurate a description as you can to a fellow student and see if he can recognise the shape from your description of it.

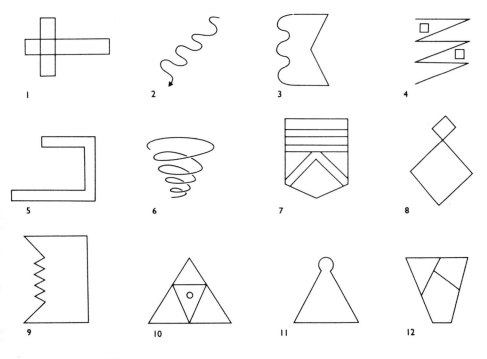

Exercise 13

Choose one of the shapes above, *or* draw a shape of your own, then show your description to a fellow student. Do not let him see the drawing. Let him attempt to draw the shape from your description of it. If he is in real difficulty, you can help him by *writing* some additions to your description.

Vocabulary guide: static description

above	upper	front
below	higher	back
	lower	rear
over		upside down
underneath		inverted
at the front	on top of	inside
at the back	at the top of	within
	at the foot/base/	outside
	bottom of	
		shapes
to the right	beside	circle
to the left	alongside	square
		triangle
on the right-hand	on one side . . .	rectangle
side		
on the left-hand side	on the other side	spiral
		serrated ⎫
		⎬(edge)
in the middle	shaped like . . .	jagged ⎭
	attached to	V-shaped
near	leading to	straight
close to	supporting	sloping
	fitting into	slanting (line)
apart	covering	diagonal
away		wavy
some distance from		

Process description

Two very common kinds of process description are describing a) how to do something, and b) how something works.

In describing *how to do something* the main thing is to arrange the information so that the process can be done straight through without unnecessary interruptions. In describing how to repair something, for example, it is best to list all the tools needed beforehand, so that the workman does not have to go away in the middle of the job to look for a hammer or a saw! As well as being *orderly*, remember that your description should be *clear, accurate* and *complete*.

Exercise 14

Imagine that an English friend has written to you that he has been given a scholarship to go to study in your country. Write to him to tell him what preparations he has to make for the journey (e.g. passports, visas (if necessary), inoculations, travellers' cheques, packing, etc). Try to get the various steps in *the right order* and give him some idea of how long he has to allow for various things to be done.

Exercise 15

Have you ever changed a punctured tyre? Or mended a fuse? Or cooked a favourite dish? Or arranged a dance? Think of any practical task that you can do and explain as clearly as you can how it is done. You may use diagrams to help make your meaning clear.

In explaining *how something works*, the procedure is very similar to the other kinds of description. Your description must be *orderly*. It might be a good idea to start by explaining the *purpose* of what you are describing, if that is not obvious. You might also describe the *basic principle* involved. The basic principle of a camera, for example, is light going through a shutter and landing on a film that is sensitive to light; the basic principle of the jet engine is that something can be made to move forwards if you can make it squirt a jet of air or water backwards, and so on. The basic principle must be clearly understood, otherwise the details will just confuse the reader. The description should also be *clear, accurate* and *complete*.

Exercise 16

Study the passage below and the diagrams beneath it until you are satisfied that you know how a simple box camera operates.

How a simple box camera works

The purpose of a camera is to take photographs, to have a permanent record on film of a scene, a friend's face or whatever. When a light-sensitive film is exposed to light for a certain period of time, an image can be recorded on the film. A box camera is simply a box which will let in the correct amount of light for the image to be recorded.

At the front of the camera is a glass lens which projects or throws the image onto a film which is stretched out at the other (back) end of the camera. Just behind the lens is a metal shutter. This can be opened for a very short period of time by pushing a lever called the 'shutter release'. The shutter will let in only the correct amount of light. The box camera is made so that no other light from any other source can come onto the film.

At the top of the camera, there is a piece of glass called the 'viewfinder' which is linked to a sort of small glass 'window' at the front of the camera, on the same side as the lens. This means that by looking through the viewfinder, the photographer can see what picture is going to be taken through the lens.

After a photograph has been taken, the film is wound on by turning the film winder knob at the side. When this has been done, a fresh piece of film is ready to be exposed.

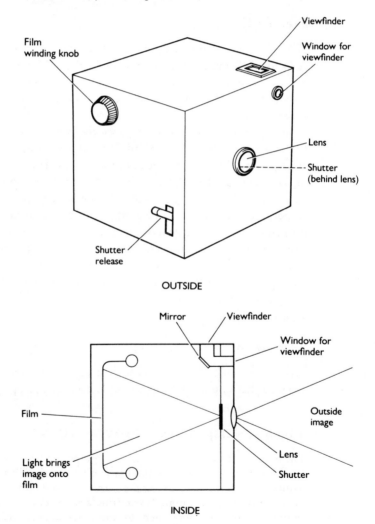

Operation of a simple box camera

How has the writer ordered or organised his description? Cover the explanation and, using the diagrams to help you with the vocabulary, write an explanation of how a box camera works. Note: do *not* try to memorise the original passage. There is nothing wrong with explaining the process in your own way.

Exercise 17

Study the passage below and the diagram alongside it until you are satisfied that you know how new laws are brought into being by the British Parliament.

How Parliament makes new laws

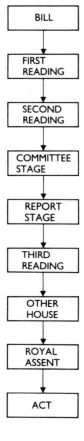

New laws can start in either the House of Lords or the House of Commons. They are usually proposed by the Government although they may be proposed by ordinary members. A law which is being proposed is called a 'Bill' until it is passed; then it becomes an 'Act' of Parliament.

The Bill first of all goes through its *first reading*. This just means that the title of the Bill is announced and a time is set for it to be discussed. The *second reading* is really a debate. The Bill may be rejected at this stage. If it is an important Bill this may cause the government to resign. On the other hand, it may be passed, or there may be no vote. If this happens, it goes on to the *committee stage* where a small group of members (perhaps between 30 and 50) meet and discuss it in detail. (For certain important Bills the whole House can turn itself into a committee which means that the detailed discussion is carried on by all the members.) When the committee has finished its work it reports the Bill, with all the changes that have been made, to the House. The Bill is discussed again at this stage and more changes can be made. This is called the *report stage*. Then the Bill is taken for its *third reading* which is a debate, just like the second reading. A vote is taken and the Bill is either passed or rejected. If it is passed, it goes to the 'other house' – i.e. not the one it was started in. So if the Bill started in the House of Commons, it would go at this point to the House of Lords.

When the Bill has been passed by both Houses, it goes to the Queen for the *Royal Assent*. A Bill may not become law until the Royal Assent has been given, but this does not mean that the Queen decides on what will become law and what will not. It is understood that the Queen will always accept Bills which have been passed by both Houses. When the Queen gives her assent, the Bill becomes an Act, and everyone that it affects must obey the new law.

How has the writer ordered his description? Cover the explanation and, with the diagram only to help you, write an explanation of how new laws are made in Britain.

Exercise 18

Think of something else which involves a process and explain how it works. If you can't think of anything, here are some suggestions:

1 *Technology*: telescope, microscope, aeroplane, submarine, lighthouse, fountain pen, telephone, radar, car engine.
2 *Social organisation*: marriage ceremony, initiation ceremony, religious ceremony, committee meeting, club dance, picnic.
3 *Natural process*: weather processes (winds, rainfall), plant respiration, cultivation of crops.

Cause and effect

In discussing cause and effect we are discussing *why* things happen. For example, look at this sentence:

'John ran to the station because he wanted to be on time for the train.'

John's wish to be on time for the train is the *cause*; his running to the station is the *effect*. Another example, look at these sentences:

'How did James come to break his leg?'
'He slipped on a banana skin.'

What is the cause and what is the effect of this example?

Simple and complex causes
A mistake often made by students writing essays is that there can only be one explanation (cause) of what they are trying to explain. In the examples we have looked at, this is in fact true. Each effect had one cause. But (of course) one effect may be due to several causes. Take a question like: 'Why was American industry located in the north of the United States rather than in the south on the eve of the Civil War?' There are probably several causes for this effect. So if you are asked to explain why something happened, do not be content with the first explanation that occurs to you. There may be others. One may also have one cause related to several effects. Remember, too, that some causes or effects may be more important than others.

(simple cause)   cause ——————————— effect

                             cause₁ ╲
(complex cause)   cause₂ ————————————→ effect
                             cause₃ ╱

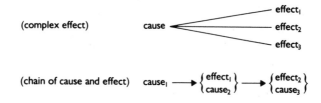

(complex effect)   cause $\longleftarrow$ effect₁ effect₂ effect₃

(chain of cause and effect)   cause₁ $\longrightarrow$ {effect₁ cause₂} $\longrightarrow$ {effect₂ cause₃}

Exercise 19

Can you answer these questions, or find out the answer to them?
Which of these questions would you say involve
a) simple cause
b) complex cause
c) complex effect
d) chain of cause and effect?

1 Why did cities in olden times have high walls round them?
2 Why can a man jump higher on the moon than he can on earth?
3 Why do we sometimes see rainbows in the sky?
4 Why do winds usually blow on-shore (i.e. from the sea) during the day, and off-shore (i.e. towards the sea) at night?
5 In developing countries, millions of people are crowding into the cities from the countryside. Have you any explanation for this?
6 Why are men usually more prominent in public life than women, even in 'advanced' societies?
7 Can you justify the amount of time and money being spent on scientific research? (Answer may be 'yes' or 'no', but you must give *reasons*.)
8 What do you think would happen if a law were passed saying that everyone should earn the same amount of money, irrespective of what he did?
9 The printing press was invented in the fifteenth century in Europe. What would you say have been the main consequences of that invention for ordinary people?
10 What would you say was the most important invention or discovery of the last few hundred years? In what ways has it affected people's lives?

Vocabulary guide: cause and effect

because	consequently
since	in consequence
	as a result
the reason is that	and so
the explanation is that	

this explains why . . .	consequent
for that/this reason	resulting from
on that account	owing to
on account of	due to

the |effect / result / outcome| (of this) was . . .

Definition

When you are writing on a topic, ask yourself if there is any important word in the topic which ought to be clearly defined to avoid confusion.

There are at least four ways of defining:

a) BY USE OR QUALITY
For example:
An *axe* is used for cutting wood.
A *tiger* has black and orange stripes and is mostly found in India.

b) BY CATEGORY
This is usually combined with use or quality to give a fuller, more meaningful definition, as in this pattern:

(*Name*)	(*Category*)	(*Use/Quality*)
An axe	is a kind of tool	used for cutting wood.
A tiger	is an animal	with black and orange stripes. It is mostly found in India.

We can sometimes use a broad category (such as *an animal*) or a narrower category (such as *a member of the cat family*), depending on what we think will help the reader.

Exercise 20

Define the following things, using the pattern above:

spade	sculptor	spear	surgeon
hammer	kitchen	snake	novel

c) BY EXAMPLE
This is a rather loose way of defining, by simply giving examples of the sort of thing you have in mind, e.g. chairs, tables, sofas, wardrobes – these are all examples of what we mean by *furniture*.

Exercise 21

Define the following by using examples:

reptile	domestic animal
crop (in agriculture)	hobby/pastime
mineral (what is mined)	gem (precious stone)
profession	traditional custom

d) BY NEGATIVE DEFINITION

It is sometimes necessary to define what you do *not* mean, in case there is any confusion, e.g.

By 'patriot' I do *not* mean someone who says, 'My country right or wrong'. By 'patriot', I mean a lover of his country who will defend it to the death when it is right, but will also be the first to criticise it when it is wrong.

The first sentence is a negative definition; what sort of definition is it in the second sentence?

Exercise 22

Use negative definition, or any other kind of definition, to distinguish between any *three* of the following:

1 friend/acquaintance	4 knowledge/wisdom
2 profession/trade	5 heroism/foolhardiness
3 liberty/license	6 flower/weed

A good definition may use only one of the methods we have used, or it may use all four. Remember that there are some things (such as *axe*, *tiger* etc) which are easily defined in a way that most people will agree with, and others (such as *democracy*, *freedom* etc) where many definitions are possible.

Exercise 23

In this exercise we look at some words which are 'difficult' as far as definition is concerned. Try defining some of them, and see how far your definition agrees with those of the other members of the class. You may wish to add some of your own words to the list.

democracy	happiness
freedom	true love
progress	good taste
civilisation	friendship
a good education	nationalism

What methods did you use to make your definitions?

Vocabulary guide: definition

to understand by (a word)	essentially
to take (a word) to mean	really
this word means/signifies	the gist/essence of the word
the meaning of this word	in the true/real sense of the
in another sense	word
alternatively	that is
distinguishing features	namely
distinctive features	in other words
main features	by . . . I do *not* mean
	not to be confused with
	is to be/must be distinguished
	from

Implication and inference

Very often an essay title takes the form of a statement or
quotation, which you are asked to discuss. Sometimes these are
very straightforward, and their meaning is plain. At other times,
you may have to think about what the statement or quotation
implies, as well as its obvious meaning.

Look at the following quotation. (*Hansard* is the official record
of all the speeches made in the House of Commons.)

'I read *Hansard* to get to sleep, and sometimes I get to sleep
more quickly than at other times.' (Mr David Crouch, M.P.,
quoted in *The Observer*, 20/3/77)

This quotation is making a statement about how Mr Crouch gets
to sleep; but the point of the statement is not what it *says*, but
what it *implies*. It implies that Parliamentary speeches are boring
(they send Mr Crouch to sleep) and sometimes very boring
(sometimes he gets to sleep more quickly than at other times).

Do not confuse *imply* and *infer*. See how they are used:

The quotation/speaker *implies* ⎤
                  ⎬ that Parliamentary speeches are
The reader *infers*   ⎦ boring.

Exercise 24

What do you think these quotations *imply*? Putting it another
way, what do you *infer* from them? (Look at the vocabulary
guide to see the different ways in which you can express
implication/inference.)

1 'It is very easy to give up smoking. I've done it dozens of times.' (Mark Twain)
2 'It is not easy to find the relatives of a poor man.' (Menander)
3 'In love, there is always one who kisses, and one who offers the cheek.' (French proverb)
4 What does the following saying imply about the difference between *art* and *science*?
   'Art is I; Science is We.' (George Bernard Shaw)
5 What do you infer from this saying about what the gipsies think of the law?
   'May you have a lawsuit in which you know you are in the right.' (Gipsy curse)

Vocabulary guide: implication and inference
imply: the author/this statement implies . . .
infer: we can infer from this statement . . .

implication	implicit	hint at
inference	understood	insinuate (something unpleasant)

by implication	gather from
presumably	take to imply

Illustration

A discussion can be much more interesting and easier to follow if it has plenty of good *examples*. Examples can be used in at least two ways:
i) to explain something abstract or difficult by giving a concrete example:
    'By *the force of gravity* we mean the force which attracts two masses to one another, and especially the force which attracts other masses towards the mass of the earth. For example, when an apple falls from a tree to the ground, it is because of the force of the earth's gravity.'
ii) to support an argument by giving examples:
    'Revolutions which overthrow despotic governments by violent means often end by establishing another kind of despotism. A good example is the French Revolution of 1789, which began as an expression of democratic will, and ended by establishing Napoleon as Emperor of the French.' (By the way, note that giving a few examples does not mean that you have proven your argument! It is sometimes possible that you have ignored *counter-examples* – the American Revolution of 1776 might be a case in point for the passage just quoted.)

Exercise 25

Write a paragraph supporting or denying two of the following arguments, using examples to do so.

1 Material prosperity does not necessarily mean a happy and peaceful society.
2 Women are not fitted to hold high political posts.
3 Animals can show behaviour that is something like intelligence.
4 The world need not depend only on fossil fuels such as oil and coal: other sources of power are or could be available.

Exercise 26

Imagine that you have to explain three of the following ideas to a school-child. Use examples to make your explanation clear. (It may be useful to have a dictionary handy for this exercise.) The subject area of the idea to be explained is in brackets.

1   (economics) inflation
2   (social studies) superstition
3   (biology) amphibians
4   (communications) codes or cyphers
5   (science) experiment
6   (history of ideas) the difference between *invention* and *discovery*
7   (politics) peace treaty
8   (biology) evolution
9   (medicine) inoculation
10 (business studies) insurance

Analogy

By *analogy* we mean comparing one thing to something else. As with examples, analogies are usually used to explain something or make it clearer. For example, if I were explaining to someone what a *computer* was I might say that it is 'a kind of mechanical or artificial brain'. This may give him an idea of the sort of thing that a computer can do.

Sometimes analogies are used in arguments (just as examples are) but this is very dangerous, as you can never *prove* anything by analogy. Look at this argument:

'The people of a country are just like the members of one family. The President is *therefore* like the head of the family. Children should not speak of their parents disrespectfully so, *therefore*, the citizens of the country should not speak of their President disrespectfully.'

What the author is saying may or may not be true, but he is wrong to use *therefore* in the second and third sentences. The people of a country may be like a family in some ways, but also unlike one in others – you cannot *prove* anything from an analogy.

Exercise 27

Here are some possible analogies. Pick two or three of them and say a) in what ways the analogy is a good one b) in what ways the analogy breaks down or is not appropriate.

1 A nation is just like a large family.
2 Life is like a game of football.
3 Religion is the opium of the people. (*Opium* is a habit-forming drug.)
4 Workers in modern society think that they are free but really they are just slaves – wage-slaves.
5 If so many people say that Mr Smith the grocer cheats his customers, there must be some truth in it. After all, where there's smoke, there's fire.
6 The democratic system of government is the most inefficient. Which would you prefer to travel on: a ship under the command of a captain, or a ship where the crew met every so often and voted on what they should do next?

Let us suppose that a child has asked you to explain why there is 'day' and 'night', and why it is 'night-time' in Britain when it is 'day-time' in Australia. How would you explain it? Can you think of any useful analogies or examples that might make your explanation clearer?

Vocabulary guide: illustration

for example	similarly
for instance	correspondingly
(be) a case in point	in the same way
a case in point is . . .	by the same token
such as	
be analogous to	can/could be compared to
comparable	to make a comparison
similar	between X and Y.
	to draw an analogy between X and Y

Evidence

Whatever point of view you take up, it is very important to support it with evidence. The evidence may be of different kinds e.g. research that you have done, quotation from an authority (writer) on the subject, cause and effect, etc.

In this section, we are going to look at a very common kind of use of evidence: *induction*.

By induction, we mean conclusions which come from experience. When we prove something by using a scientific experiment, then we are using *induction*. If we boil several cans of water and observe what happens, we may say that above a certain temperature (100°C, in fact) water turns into steam. If several of my friends are involved in accidents while riding motor-cycles, then I may conclude that riding a motor-cycle is a dangerous thing to do. In other words, we have a *sample* of events, and we *draw conclusions* from the sample.

Exercise 28

How would you prove or disprove the following statements? How certain would you be about the results?
1 Water freezes at 0°C (32°F).
2 Malaria is caused by mosquito bites.
3 Students remember something that is meaningful better than something which is not.
4 Being overweight is one of the causes of heart disease.
5 People with training in science or technology would make better administrators/managers than arts graduates.

One can easily make mistakes in induction. For example:
a) the sample may be too small.
b) the sample may not be typical (those friends of mine who were involved in motor cycle accidents may all have been very careless people).
c) the sample may be irrelevant (i.e. have little or nothing to do with the subject).
d) the fact that one thing happens after another does not mean to say that it was caused by it.
e) the fact that two things occur at the same time does not mean to say that they are connected.
f) an effect may have more than one cause.

Exercise 29

What do you think of the evidence for these arguments?

1 You have a better chance of being famous if you are small in height. Look at Napoleon – he was a small man, yet he became Emperor of the French.

2 Happenings on earth are controlled by the stars. A comet appeared in the sky just before the assassination of Julius Caesar.

3 If you want proof of the harmful effects of TV, consider this: statistics have shown that as the amount of violence on television has increased, so has the amount of violent crime in real life.

4 There is no doubt that the Welsh are a musical people. There are five Welshmen in our choir, and they all have excellent voices.

5 The preacher was attempting to show to the meeting that alcohol was very bad for people to drink. He dropped a worm into a jar of alcohol. The worm soon curled up and died.

6 A drunk man at the meeting said that it proved that, if you suffered from worms, you should drink alcohol!

7 The English word *malaria* comes from two Italian words *mal aria* meaning 'bad air'. It was noticed that people who suffered from malaria usually lived near marshy (muddy, swampy) ground, and that therefore malaria was caused by the 'bad air' from the marches.

8 Badminton is one of the most popular sports in Britain. If you don't believe me, just ask anyone in any badminton club.

Discussion

Discussion is the most common type of essay and also the most complex. It is complex because it can involve many different kinds of activities, including some of the activities we have been looking at: listing, narrative, description, definition, and use of evidence. In the exercise which follows you will be given a chance to analyse the discussion process for yourself.

Exercise 30

First pick a topic for discussion. Each member of the group should make a suggestion. The group should choose one or more of the topics and write them up in a short discussion paper. When you have finished, exchange the papers or (if there is time) read some of them aloud. As you are reading the paper or

listening to it, look at the check-list below. Add any other criteria
to the list which you think important.

Discuss your comments with the writer/speaker.

Keep the check-list handy and use it later for any discussion
papers you have to write.

Criteria

1 Has the writer (speaker) stated the problem clearly?
2 Has he defined all the important *terms* (words) which ought to
   be defined?
3 Does he support his argument with *evidence*?
4 Is the evidence *relevant*?
5 Has he made good use of *examples*?
6 Has he used *analogy* correctly, i.e. to clarify and not to mislead?
7 Has he avoided mistakes in reasoning (like those illustrated in
   exercise 29)?
8 Has he made his own point of view clear?

Glossary of D-words often used in essay titles and examination questions

Note: The explanations given for these words can be a *rough guide
only*. You must always go by the total meaning of the title or
question. Read the question *carefully*: do not jump to conclusions
about what is required on the basis of the D-words only.

Account: a) (usually in phrases as *give an account of/a brief account of*)
describe. *Brief account* indicates, of course, that not too much time
should be spent on the description. b) *account for:* give the reason(s)
for.

Apply (to): put something to use, show how something can be
used in a particular situation. The 'something' that is to be applied
may be a theory, or certain findings, data, results of research, etc.

Comment (on): give you views on something, say what you think
about something. This D-word is often used with a quotation or
statement: you are expected to give your own reaction to it
(views on it). Do you agree with the statement or not? What are
your reasons?

Compare (with): say in what ways two (or more) things are like
each other, resemble each other. Sometimes includes the idea of
contrast (see below).

Consider: describe and give your thoughts on.

Contrast (with): say in what ways two (or more) things are
different from each other.

Describe: say what something is like, how it works, and so on.

Devise: think up, work out a plan, solution to a problem, etc. Often used for some practical problem that has to be overcome.

Discuss: give your thoughts on something, say what you think about a particular thing. Sometimes *discuss* can mean little more than 'state what you know about . . .', but usually it also involves giving your own ideas, or giving evidence that you have thought about a topic and not just memorised certain facts. N.B. It is wrong to say *discuss about*.

Evaluate: decide the worth of something; judge; decide how good, bad, worthwhile, relevant, important, etc, something is. Sometimes relates to comparing certain things and deciding which is best.

Explain: a) *explain why:* give the reason for, cause of something. Often another way of saying *why . . .?* b) *explain how:* describe (a process) clearly.

Identify: put a name to, list something.

Indicate: point out; does not usually involve giving very much detail.

List: make a list of a number of things. Usually involves simply remembering or finding out a number of things and putting them down one after the other; but it is often better if you make your list according to some kind of system.

Plan: think out how something is to be done, made, organised, etc. You usually have to show that you can think your way into a problem, foresee difficulties, and think of practical situations.

Report (on): describe what one has seen or done. Usually refers to something which one has experienced directly (personally). Also *give/make a report on.*

Review: write a report on something. Sometimes it involves both stating what the facts are and also saying what your own opinions are.

Specify: give the details of something. Usually involves being specific, i.e. precise, accurate.

State: say clearly.

Work out: find a solution to a problem, etc.

Presentation

Typescript or manuscript? One decision you will have to make is whether your essay is going to be presented in typed form (*typescript*). If it is a major piece of work you should seriously consider having it typed. Minor essays can usually be presented in handwritten form (*manuscript*) – but remember, your handwriting must be legible!

There are other points which you should bear in mind:
1   Use good quality paper of a reasonable size, and preferably with a margin (lined A4 is usually a good size paper to use for handwritten essays).
2   Have a first page on which you have the basic information on the essay (see example opposite).
3   With a longer essay it is a good idea to put a summary or 'abstract' at the beginning. Also, longer essays should have section headings listed at the beginning.
4   To protect your work, you can put it in a folder with your name and class/group on the outside.
5   Leave plenty of space for your tutor's comments. Leave a margin of at least one inch (2.5 cm) on one side.
6   Number the pages of the essay.

Exercise 1

Put yourself in the place of a tutor who has just received a piece of work. Below is a list of some aspects of presenting an essay. Say whether you would be 'pleased' by each quality, or 'annoyed', or neither.
1   The student's name is not on the essay.
2   The essay seems to be far outside the recommended length.
3   The student has used paper with a margin.
4   The essay is written on very small sheets of notepaper.
5   The writing is very difficult to read.
6   The essay is protected by being put inside a folder.
7   The student does not indicate anywhere what it is that he is trying to prove or show.

8 The student gives no indication of what books (if any) he has consulted.
9 The student quotes from a book but does not show clearly that it is a quotation and *not* his own idea.
10 The student quotes from a book and gives an exact reference so that the tutor can check it for himself.
11 The essay is illustrated with clear, relevant and helpful charts, diagrams, tables etc.
12 The front page of the essay is decorated with complicated designs.

Exercise 2

Read the summary on p. 158, which relates to the essay whose first page is shown below, and then answer the questions which follow.

```
M.M. Faez                    Tutor: Mr Green



(Class) BA1
(Group) C


       (Subject) Linguistics:

         Term I Major essay


   Discuss the Sapir-Whorf hypothesis
   that the way in which we think is
   determined by the language we
   speak.          (2,500 words)


   Actual length:   approx 2,700 words.



 Submitted: 2/11/80
```

Sample front page of an essay

Summary

```
In this essay, I am going to argue that Sapir
and Whorf are overstating their case when they
say that the particular language we speak determines
the way that we think.  I shall suggest a weaker
case.  I shall argue that a particular language
influences the thoughts of a speaker, in that
certain ideas are more 'available' (i.e. easier
for him to think of) than others; but also that
it is a relatively simple matter for a speaker to
overcome this tendency and to follow new ways of
thought while still operating in his own native
language.
```

1 The essay is about whether a certain view of language held by two famous scholars (Sapir and Whorf) is true or not. What is the student doing in the first sentence – is he accepting their view or not?
2 What is the student doing in the second and third sentences – is he giving more evidence for the Sapir–Whorf view, or is he explaining his own point of view?
3 Assuming that this is an example of a good summary, what does it tell you about the sort of thing that should appear in a good summary?
4 The length of the summary is less than 100 words. How does this compare with the length of the essay?
5 What would you say are the advantages of preparing a summary for an essay?

Sources and references

You must be very careful when you are writing an essay to make it clear when the words or ideas that you are using are your own and when they are taken from another writer.

There are two ways in which you can refer to another person's ideas: a) by reporting; b) by direct quotation.

Reporting
This simply means putting the other writer's ideas in your own words. Sometimes people report ideas rather than use direct quotation because it means that you can summarise at the same time. Here is an example:

```
In an essay entitled 'An American Indian model of the
universe'[1], Whorf argues that the language of the
Hopi Indians forces them to think about many things
(measuring the passage of time, for example) in a
completely different way from people speaking a
European language.
```

. . . .

```
[1]Whorf (1956), pp. 57-64.
```

Here we see that the student who wrote this paragraph has
summarised the article he is referring to; but that he has made it
clear from whom and where he has got the ideas he is discussing.

Direct quotation
Occasionally it is necessary to quote the author's own words. If
you find yourself making a very long quotation, ask yourself
whether it would not be a better idea to report the author's ideas
in your own words.

When you are referring to a writer it is normal to refer to him
by his second name (e.g. 'Dickens says . . .'), or sometimes by his
full name e.g. ('Charles Dickens wrote . . .'), but *never* by his first
name alone. If the writer is still living it is possible (but not
necessary) to put his title in front (e.g. 'Professor Brown writes
. . .').

Here is an example of the use of quotation from a student's
essay:

```
In his essay entitled 'An American Indian model of
the universe', Whorf states quite categorically,
'After long and careful study and analysis, the
Hopi Language is seen to contain no words,
grammatical forms, constructions or expressions
that refer directly to what we call "time", and
to past, present, or future...' [1]
```

. . . .

```
[1] Whorf (1956), p.57.
```

You can see that the writer's words are within single quotation
marks. The quotation is preceded by a comma, or sometimes by

a colon (:). If, however, the quotation is a word or a short phrase, it may just be written as part of the sentence it appears in, but always with single quotation marks.

You must quote the words *exactly*, except

a) where the writer you are quoting himself uses quotation marks. Then you must change his single quotation marks into double quotation marks. Of course, if the original text has double quotation marks, you will keep them. The main thing is to distinguish between the author's quotation marks and your own.

b) where there is some material which is not relevant and which you want to omit. You indicate that you have omitted something by putting a series of three dots. (In the example, the sentence is not quoted to the end, and this is shown by the series of dots.)

c) where there is a reference etc which is not clear. You can put in some information of your own in *square* brackets. This usually happens with pronouns like *he*, *this* etc. For example:

```
'In particular, he [the Hopi Indian] has no general
notion or intuition of TIME as a smooth flowing
continuum...' 1
```

· ·

---

1 Whorf (1956), p.57

Exercise 3

Below is a selection of quotations. Write them in the way that you would quote them, if you had occasion to do so. Follow the instructions carefully. There is an example to show you what to do, and some useful phrases at the end. In this exercise there is no need to mention any publishing details except the author and the date of publication. The date of publication is always put in brackets, e.g. Packard (1960).

Example. Quote what the author has to say about 'the working class' in the United States.

THE WORKING CLASS. The heads of families of this class frequently have not finished high school. They work steadily, in good times, at jobs that require little training and can be mastered in a few days or, at most, a few weeks. (Vance Packard: *The Status Seekers*, Longmans, 1960)

Answer. Packard (1960) has this to say about the working class in the United States: 'The heads of families of this class frequently have not finished high school. They work steadily, in good times, at jobs that require little training and can be mastered in a few days or, at most, a few weeks.'

1 Quote what the author has to say about 'the real upper class' in the United States.
   THE REAL UPPER CLASS. These are the people who are likely to be on the board of directors of local industries, banks, universities and community chests; who send their daughters to finishing schools and their sons, probably, to a boarding school and, certainly, to a 'good' college. (Vance Packard: *The Status Seekers,* Longmans, 1960)

2 Make a direct quotation.
   In work with maladjusted children it is necessary to break down barriers between adults and children. (Margaret Branch and Aubrey Cash: *Gifted Children*, Souvenir Press, 1966)

3 Make a direct quotation. (Since you are quoting out of context, there is one word you would probably miss out – what is it?)
   Certainly the spectacular flights of U.S. astronauts into space – like the similar successes in the U.S.S.R. – are proof that elaborate achievements in science and engineering not so long ago recorded as impossible have now become matters of routine. (Barry Commoner: *Science and Survival*, Ballantine Books, 1970)

4 Make a direct quotation. Make it clear to any reader that the author is referring to rural primary school leavers in developing countries. (Again, since the passage is being quoted out of context there is a word you would probably miss out.)
   They therefore move to the town in search of manual or clerical employment appropriate, in their own estimation, to their new qualifications. (Peter C. Lloyd: *Classes, Crises and Coups*, MacGibbon & Kee, 1971)

5 Report the author's argument. She suggests one reason why women might find it difficult to get promotion. Briefly *report* the reason in your own words as far as possible.
   Most working women agree that women are by no means always helped by the attitudes of other women. For the more successful career women there is a certain satisfaction in being one of the few women moving in a masculine world. Such a position can provide powerful compensations to sexually unsuccessful women who find it attractive and flattering to be regarded by male colleagues as different from other women. This type of satisfaction depends on scarcity value, and such women may well subconsciously be unwilling to alter this personally satisfying state of affairs. So far from promoting

opportunities for other women, they may in fact positively block them.   (Nancy Seear: 'The position of women in industry', in the collection *Men and Work in Modern Britain*, ed. David Weir, Fontana/Collins, 1973)

career woman: woman who is devoted full-time to a career in business, the professions etc.
scarcity value: being highly regarded or valued because there are not many of them.
subconsciously: without deliberately meaning to do so.
so far from: instead of.

Useful phrases
As X points out . . .
X tells/shows us that . . .
X draws it to our attention that . . .
To quote from X . . .
In a book/article entitled . . .
X makes the point that . . .
It was X who first said . . .
X suggests/states . . .
Referring to . . . , X says that . . .

Footnotes and references

There are two reasons for having footnotes:
1 To give details of a source. (See pp. 159 and 160 above for examples of this.) The simplest way of referring to a source is by using the author's name and the date in which the book or article was published, e.g. Whorf (1956). You can then give all the other necessary details in the list of references at the end. (If you are cross-referring to your own essay, put 'See page (section etc)' followed by the number and 'above' or 'below'.
2 To give extra information about a topic. As a general rule, try to avoid this kind of footnote. If what you have to say is relevant, fit it into the main part of the text. If it is not relevant, miss it out.

There are certain abbreviations which writers sometimes use in footnotes and quotations. They are listed for reference on pp. 169–70 below.

List of references (Bibliography)
You *must* make a list of all the books that you have read or referred to in writing your essay – but don't put down any you

have not read! Bibliographies are listed alphabetically by author with title, publisher and date.

Here is an example of a bibliography with some comments on it. Study the example and then do exercise 4.

Bibliography

Anderson, Wallace L. and Stageburg, Norman C. (eds.)[1] (1966)[2] *Introductory Readings on Language*. Holt, Rinehart and Winston, New York

Black, Max (ed.) (1962) *The Importance of Language*. Prentice Hall, New Jersey

Hamp, Eric P., and others[3] (eds.) (1966) *Readings in Linguistics*. University of Chicago Press, Chicago and London

Hayakawa, S. I. (1965) *Language in Thought and Action*. Allen and Unwin, London

Sapir, Edward (1949) *Selected Writings of Edward Sapir in Language, Culture and Personality* (ed. David G. Mandelbaum).[4] Cambridge University Press, Cambridge

Whorf, Benjamin Lee (1956) *Language, Thought and Reality: Selected Writings of B. L. Whorf* (ed. John B. Carroll). Chapman and Hall, London[5]

Notes:

1 (eds.) means editors. The book is listed under the surname of the first editor. Note that the surname of the writers is put first to make it easier to follow the alphabetical sequence.

2 This is a bibliography in which the student has been referring to books by *author* (or *editor*) and *date*: so these two things come first.

3 Where there are more than two editors or authors you can simply put 'and others' after naming the first one.

4 In this book all the writings are by one man (Sapir), so it is listed under his name, and the editor's name comes later.

5 This is the book that has been referred to several times already in this unit. Note that Whorf (1956) refers to the date that the book was published – it does not refer to the time he wrote (or even first published) the quotation, which was in fact more than twenty years earlier.

Exercise 4

Below is a bibliography submitted by a student who has written an essay on British professional life. Although it is a short bibliography, the student has made *four* mistakes. Can you spot them?

Bibliography

Jackson, J.A. (ed.) (1970)   Professions and
  Professionalism.   Cambridge University Press,
  Cambridge

Elliott, Philip (1972)   The Sociology of the
  Professions.   London

Gerstl, J.E. and Hutton, S.P. (1966)   Engineers:
  The Anatomy of a Profession.   Tavistock Publications,
  London

A.H. Halsey, and M. Trow   (1971)   The British
  Academics.   Faber, London

Zander, M.   Lawyers and the Public Interest.
  Weidenfeld & Nicolson, London

(See Appendix, p. 216 for a correct form of this bibliography.)

Exercise 5

Think of six books connected with your subject. Write them out in the form of a bibliography. (Make sure you have all the publishing details correct.)

Revising the essay

Most students writing an important essay will want to do it in at least two stages (maybe more). We shall call the two stages:
a) draft version
b) final version.
  When you are writing your draft, your main concern is *to get it down on paper*. Don't worry too much about spelling, grammar or style at this stage. Let nothing interrupt the flow of ideas – but remember to leave plenty of space between the lines and in the margin for corrections. When you have finished your draft, you should check it *separately* for:
a) general sense
b) details: grammar, spelling, punctuation, style etc.

Exercise 6

When correcting a typescript, use correction symbols that are easily understood. Here is a passage from a student's essay. There are quite a number of mistakes, both general and detailed. They have, however, been corrected. See if you can follow the corrections and write out the passage correctly. (You may find the table of correction symbols on p. 168 useful.)

Many people say that the 'industrial age' is past and that we are now in the 'post-industrial age'. Indeed it is true that modern technology (especially computerisation) ensures that the ability to produce is limited only by the supply of materials and energy supply. It said that in the post-industrial age the capacity to produce has far exceeded the demand for goods.

We can confidently expect that both of these problems will be overcome in the next century as synthetic cheap materials are devised and as renewable fuel resources are developed (e.g. solar power, nuclear fusion etc.) then we can expect an enormous leap in wealth and the life-style enjoyed by only a small elite today will be accessible to many.

Checking for general sense
Read through the whole essay to check that:
a) the general meaning is clear.
b) the ideas follow naturally from one another.
c) there is no irrelevance.
d) nothing has been left out by accident.

Exercise 7

Below is a short essay on the effects of tourism. Read through it *for general sense* and make any appropriate changes. (When you have finished check your version against the correct version in the Appendix, p. 216.)

The effects of tourism

Tourism is one of the great growth industries of the last few decades. In most countries there are official organisations to encourage tourists; and some countries even have Ministries of Tourism, so important is this activity. In fact, very often the ordinary people are worse off because the presence of large numbers of tourists means that the price of food becomes too expensive for poorer people.

There are two main arguments for tourism. It is usually people from better-off countries that can afford to travel, and they bring with them much-needed 'hard currency'. The first, and most obvious one, is the economic benefits which come to the host country. The second argument is that tourism increases 'international understanding' and friendship between peoples of different countries. I went to Spain on holiday last year and thoroughly enjoyed it.

But are the effects of tourism all good ones? I doubt it. Let us look at the economic argument first. Who are the people who actually benefit from tourism? Not the mass of people, I am sure.

My conclusion is that tourism is a harmful development and should be discouraged not encouraged.

And here is another thing. Does tourism really promote 'international understanding'? Many tourists cannot even speak the languages of the countries they visit. Their wealth only makes the local people more aware of their own poverty.

Detailed marking
The second stage of correction is detailed marking. At this stage you are still very much checking that your meaning is clear, but you are especially interested in details – grammatical mistakes, spelling, punctuation and (if the essay is handwritten) places where the writing might be difficult to read: This kind of checking has to be done on the draft version, but also on the final version before you hand it in. If you have the time, it is a good idea to put the final version of the essay aside for a few days, and then to look at it with a less familiar eye. Another idea is to exchange your finished essay with someone else, since it is easier to spot someone else's mistakes than it is to see your own.

Exercise 8

Read the paragraph below. The student who wrote the paragraph has made *ten* mistakes, see if you can correct them. (You may find

the table of correction symbols on p. 168 useful.) Check your
version against the correct version in the Appendix, p. 217.
(The paragraph refers to extra-sensory perception, i.e. the ability
which some people are supposed to have to be aware of things,
but not through the normal senses of hearing, sight etc. It
therefore includes telepathy ('mind-reading') etc. The reference is
to J. Bronowski *The Ascent of Man*, B.B.C. Publications, London,
1976).

Extra-sensory perception

Why is it that so many scientists are reluctant to
explore the possibility of extra-sensory perception?
In the concluding chatper of his book The Ascent
of Man, Bronowski is sadened to discover 'in the
west ... a retreat from knowledge ... into extra-
sensory perception and mystery.'[1] Why should such
investigation be a matter for regret. In earlier
passage in same book, bronowski admit that 'whatever
fundamental units the world is put together from,
they are more delicate, more fugitive, more
startling than we catch in the butterfly net of our
senses.'[2] It may be that science will have to extend
the ragne of its investigations in order to more
significant discoveries make.

---

[1]   p. 437

[2]   p. 364

SYMBOL	EXAMPLE	COMMENT and EXPLANATION
⊘/ ∧	He bought apples ⊘∧ pears and peaches	Put in comma (question-mark etc.) The required punctuation is put in the circle.
⊙/∧ ≡	He knocked on the door and waited ⊙∧ ≡then he came in	Put a full stop after waited. Make t a capital letter (Then . . .)
←[ ]	˅Then he came in. ˅[He knocked on the door and waited.]	Shift this sentence (word, paragraph etc.) to the place indicated by the arrow.
—	*is* He ~~was~~ here now	Take out the word **was** and put in **is**
↶	He knocked on the door. He came in.↶ ⌐He strode over to the table.	Make these two paragraphs into one.
∧	*e* They belie∨d in witches.	Put in the letter **e**. (Can also be used for words.)
∪∩	He is afraid to a⌊k⌒s⌉	Transpose (switch) these two letters (words etc.)
NP/ /	He decided to wait. ᴺᴾ/Some hours later John finally arrived.	Start a new paragraph here
(stet)....	*was* (stet) He ~~is working~~ hard · · · · · · · yesterday.	Do not correct the section that has the dotted line under it – leave it as it was before the correction.

Note: These symbols are particularly useful when correcting a typed draft. With handwritten drafts simpler methods can be used.

Words and abbreviations commonly used in connection with quotations and footnotes

Note: There is a tendency for Latin words and abbreviations to be replaced by English ones; where this is possible the English equivalent is asterisked (★), and is explained more fully in the English section.

Latin

cf.	compare★
et al.	and others★ (*et* is a word; *al.* is an abbreviation).
et seq.	ff.★ (and following) (*et* is a word; *seq.* is an abbreviation).
ibid.	the same author, book/article and page; or the same author and book with the new page mentioned: *ibid.*, p. 44. Used when the writer is referring again to a book/article that he has just referred to.
infra	below★. (A word; not an abbreviation.)
loc. cit.	in the article, chapter or section that I have referred to before. The author's name must always be given: Whorf, *loc. cit.*
op. cit.	in the book that I have referred to before. The author's name and a page reference must always be given: Whorf, *op. cit.*, p. 56.
passim	here and there throughout. Used when a topic is referred to several times in a book etc, that you are referring to: Whorf (1956), pp. 56–64, *passim.* (A word, not an abbreviation.)
(sic)	this is used when you are quoting from a writer who has made an obvious mistake (usually spelling) and you want the reader to know it is not *your* mistake! Also sometimes used by writers to draw the reader's attention to something that might be considered very silly, when it almost has the meaning 'Would you believe it?' The word *sic* means 'thus' or 'so' in Latin. (A word, not an abbreviation.)
supra	above★. (A word, not an abbreviation.)

English

above	appearing earlier in the same page, article, chapter etc. (Often *see above.*)
and others	used when there are more than two authors; the first author only is named: Quirk and others: *A Grammar of Contemporary English.*

below	appearing later in the same page, article, chapter etc. (Often *see below*.)
cp., compare	used for drawing the reader's attention to some other relevant source.
ed., eds.	editor, edition; editors, editions.
ff.	and following; used to refer to the pages that come after a page referred to: Whorf (1956), p. 56 ff.
ms., mss.	manuscript; manuscripts.
n.d.	no date given.
n.p.	no place given.
n. pub.	no publisher given.
no., nos.	number; numbers.
p., pp.	page; pages.
trans.	translator; translated; translation.
vol., vols.	volume; volumes.

Unit 8 Assessment, study techniques and examinations

Do you agree or disagree with the following statement?

'Students who fail examinations study far fewer hours than students who pass.'

There is some evidence to show that this statement may be, in fact, incorrect. Malleson (1961; quoted in Allen, 1966) shows that medical students at University College, London who failed their second Bachelor of Medicine examinations studied just as long on average as those who passed. How can this be so?

Perhaps we can say this about examinations: a) You must know your subject (obviously). *But also* b) Studying for long periods of time is not enough, you must put your time to good use. This unit is intended to help you to do that.

The unit is in four sections:
Necessary information about assessment.
Study and memorisation techniques.
Before the examination.
During the examination.

You will notice that in this unit, as well as the usual *exercises*, there are also *routines* which can be applied to any course of study that you may have to do in future. (Full references for the books and articles cited are on p. 189 below.)

Necessary information about assessment

The first thing that you must find out is the *system of assessment* for each course, and each part of the course. Find out if any of the subjects are reckoned to be more important than others. Then find out *how* and *when* you are going to be assessed for each subject. Find out (if you can) the *weighting* of each assessment how important it is in the overall assessment. An example of how this information should be laid out is given below. (Get as much information about each assessment as you can. If you are told the actual topics, so much the better, but this will probably not be the case. Find out if examinations are seen or unseen, free-answer or objective etc.)

1 *Statistics*   (Must pass)
   weekly class tests
   1 project
   1 exam

Task	Term	Date due	Length	Weighting
weekly class tests	1, 2, 3	(done throughout year)	(not specified)	40%
project	1, 2, 3	21/6	(not specified)	40%
exam	3	26/6 27/6	2 × 2 hr papers (Paper I is an open (seen) paper)	20%

2 *English language*   (Must pass)
   25 weekly exercises, each of equal weight
   No exam

3 *Economics*   (Must pass)
   4 essays
   1 exam

Task	Term	Date due	Length	Weighting
essay	1	20/11	2,000 words	
essay	2	18/1	2,000 words	
essay	2	20/2	2,000 words	40%
essay	3	20/5	2,000 words	
exam	3	28/6 29/6	2 × 3 hr papers	60%

4 *Economic History*   (Elective subject: pass not essential)
   1 normal essay
   1 essay written under exam conditions

Task	Term	Date due	Length	Weighting
essay	2	22/2	1,500 words	50%
essay/exam	3	20/6	$1\frac{1}{2}$ hr paper	50%

Exercise 1

Look at the sample course assessment outline above.
1 How important is the examination at the end of the year in Statistics? (Be precise.)
2 Is there much emphasis on *memorisation* in the Economics course?
3 What difference is there between the Statistics course and Economics course in terms of the importance of the exam?
4 Are there any times when the work 'bunches', i.e. a number of essays or exams coming together?
5 How important are the weekly exercises in English Language?
6 Is there any one of the subjects in which a pass is not essential?

7 What looks like being the easiest time of the year for a student doing this course? (Assume that the course runs from October to June.)
8 When is he going to be under heavy pressure of work?
9 Is there anything he could do to relieve the pressure, e.g. by 'spreading' the work?

Course assessment outline routine

Make a note of the answers to the following points, and keep it somewhere where you can refer to it again.
1 As soon as you can, make out a course assessment outline for your own course.
2 Which subjects are you going to concentrate on, or are they all equally important?
3 What is the comparative importance (weighting) of examinations, essays, class-tests, practical work, projects, exercises, laboratory work, contribution in seminars etc?
4 Do written work and examinations bunch at any time?
5 When do you think you are going to be under most pressure?
6 What can you do to spread the load of work?

If you have a lot of written work, all to be done for different dates, you can keep track of the different tasks by making up a week-by-week 'Calendar of work'. This can also be used to keep track of your progress. The calendar could be made up two or three weeks ahead. Here is an example:

Calendar of work

Due day/date	Task	Subject	Length	Handed in	Grade
Mon. 20 Nov.	essay	Economics	2,000 words	20/11	C+
Tues. 21 Nov.	class test	Statistics	—	21/11	B
Wed. 22 Nov.	—	—	—	—	—
Thurs. 23 Nov.	exercise	English	—	23/11	C
Fri. 24 Nov.	seminar discussion	Economic History	10 min talk	—	—

Calendar of work routine

Make up a week-by-week calendar of work similar to the one above. Put in first the routine tasks which you have to do every week, e.g. weekly exercises, lab reports etc. Then fill in details of the work to be done as they become known to you. You can use a cheap desk-diary, or you can simply use a notebook, ruled off as above.

If examinations are important for any of your subjects, then you should find out as many details about each one as you can. Again, you might find it useful to make a list of them, for example:

Examination programme details

Subject	Date	Length	Number of questions to be done	Kind of exam	Area
Economic History	20/6	1½ hrs	1	essay (notes allowed)	1920–1940
Statistics I	26/6	2 hrs	4 out of 8	seen	Forecasting
Statistics II	27/6	2 hrs	4 out of 8	unseen (calculators allowed)	Interpretation of data
Economics I	28/6	3 hrs	3 out of 7	essays	Microeconomics
Economics II	29/6	3 hrs	3 out of 6	essays	Macroeconomics

Examination programme routine

Find out as early as you can
1 *When* the examinations are held.
2 What *length* they are (in hours).
3 What *kind* of examinations they are:
   a) are they the usual essay-type examinations?
   b) are they objective examinations (e.g. multiple-choice questions)?
   c) if the answer to b) is 'yes', are they computer-marked or manually marked?
   d) are they 'seen' examinations (i.e. the questions are known beforehand)?
   e) are you allowed to bring in textbooks or notes for reference?
   f) are you allowed to bring in other aids (e.g. pocket calculators)?
   g) is there any equipment you *must* bring with you?
4 What the *design* of the examination is:
   a) how many parts to the exam?
   b) how many questions in each part?
   c) how many questions must you do?
   d) are there any compulsory questions you must do?
5 What *areas* the examinations cover, e.g. practical, theoretical etc?
6 Whether previous examination papers are kept in the college or university library. Consult them *early on* in your course. It

may even be a good idea to make a copy of some recent past papers. Check them from time to time as you go through your course to see which questions you could now attempt. (This point will be taken up again below, pp. 187–8.)

The time taken up in making out these routines is time taken from your studies. Some students spend too much time 'planning' and not enough time 'doing'! On the other hand, all the routines contain information which you will have to find out at some stage during the course. It might as well be laid out systematically. It is also good for you psychologically to feel that you know exactly what you have to do.

Exercise 2

Without looking back, can you list *five* essential points that you should know about any exam?

Grading
Most colleges and universities have some kind of grading system, and you should find out what it is. This will help you to find out what your marks or grades *mean*. A mark on its own tells you very little: is 80% a bad mark or a good one? It sounds good, but what if everyone else in the class has scored over 90%? Obviously you need some sort of guide as to what is acceptable. In the case of marks, it would be useful to know the *average mark* of the class. If you are still puzzled, ask your tutor whether he thought your work was above or below average.

Similarly with grades – find out what they *mean*. One grading system might go like this:

A   Excellent
B   Good
C   Average
D   Just adequate
E   Fail

If you get an average grade it means that your tutor is satisfied with your work, but it is not outstanding. An average grade is therefore not something to be very downcast about. In fact, there is no need to be discouraged by any grade, *provided that you can learn from it.*

If you get a low grade, do not go protesting to your tutor that it should be higher. He is the expert, not you. What you *can* do is to go to him and ask his advice. How could you have improved your grade? (Of course, the tutor may have already answered this question in his comments on your work. Read them carefully before going to him; it may not be necessary to bother him.)

A low grade may be because of one of the two factors, but sometimes both:

1 *Information.* The information you have given may be
   a) wrong
   b) not enough
   c) not relevant

2 *Presentation.* The information may be presented badly, e.g.
   a) you have not answered the question.
   b) your thinking is not clear, or confused.
   c) the arguments are illogical.
   d) you have not made clear which ideas are your own and which have been taken from other people.
   e) you have not supported your arguments with evidence (either because you did not know the evidence, or you knew it but did not use it).
   f) you have not summarised your argument clearly.
   g) you have not come to any definite conclusions.

Mistakes of information are serious, because you may be asked them again in another test. Mistakes of presentation may be even more serious because you may go on making the same kind of mistake on one piece of work after another.

Analysis of assessment routine

1 When you get your essay, test etc back, note the grade or mark in your 'Calendar of work'.
2 Make sure you know what the grade etc means – is it satisfactory, or not?
3 Read the tutor's comments carefully.
4 If you have got a poor or even average grade, ask yourself whether there were
   a) mistakes in information.
   b) mistakes in presentation.
5 If there were mistakes in *information*, make sure that you find out what the facts are. Check back to your notebooks to make sure that you have not, perhaps, noted down something wrong in a lecture. Make a note of the facts for future reference.
6 If there were mistakes in *presentation*, be clear about what they were. Make a list of them. Check the list over before you do your next piece of work.
7 If you got a low grade, and if you are still *genuinely* puzzled by it, see your tutor and ask him where you have gone wrong. Make notes of what he tells you.
8 If there were genuine personal reasons why you did badly, for example if you were not well or you were worried about news

from home, you can tell your tutor. He will almost certainly not be able to change the grade or mark, but he may be able to help and advise you.

9 Having done all this, put the work behind you and get on with the next piece of work. Do not brood over bad grades. Learn from your mistakes and try to do better next time.

Exercise 3

1 Jim Brown got 40% in his last examination in Biology. Was that a bad result?

2 Jack and Jill both got a grade C for their English exercise. Does that mean that both pieces of work were of exactly the same standard?

3 Bill Jones got 70% for English and 85% for Mathematics. Which subject is he better at?

4 Look back to the 'Course assessment outline', p. 172. Let us imagine that pieces of work in this course are graded A–E, and E is a fail grade. Philip Green got an E for his first essay in Economics and also for his essay in Economic History. Does that mean that he will fail these two subjects?

5 Which of the following tutor's comments are on *information* and which on *presentation*?
   a) 'Your essay is marred by muddled thinking.'
   b) 'You have misinterpreted what Burridge has to say about myths and dreams.'
   c) 'You have summarised your reading very well, but you do not make your own position clear.'
   d) 'You could have made more use of diagrams.'
   e) 'You have not understood my definition of "managerial capitalism".'
   f) 'You have got the correct solution, but I am not clear as to how you arrived at it.'

Study and memorisation techniques

Planning your study really boils down to answering two very important questions:
1 What do you have to do?
2 How much time do you have to do it?

1 *What do you have to do?* The information you have gathered in the previous section may have given you an answer to this.

2 *How much time?* Get into the habit of thinking of *study hours* rather than calendar periods. If you say, 'I have a month to do

my next exam', you make it sound like a long time. But how many *study hours* can you devote to the exam each week? Ten ... Twenty ... Two ...? You can easily see that the calendar measurement is almost meaningless, unless you have a clear idea of what it means in *study hours*.

Exercise 4

Look at these personal timetables of two students doing the same course. (The timetables represent a typical week day, Monday–Friday; Saturdays and Sundays are free.)

BILL		JIM	
8 a.m.	Rise	8 a.m.	Rise
9–10	Economics Lecture	9–10	Economics Lecture
10–11	Coffee/Chat	10–10.30	Coffee/Chat
11–12	Sociology Lecture	10.30–11	Study
12–2	Lunch	11–12	Sociology Lecture
2–3	Statistics	12–1	Lunch
3–4	English Class	1–2	Study
4–5	Squash	2–3	Statistics
5–7	Dinner	3–4	English Class
7–8	Watch TV	4–5	Badminton
8–9	Supper/Chat	5–6.30	Dinner
9–10	Study	6.30–8	Study
10–11	Read magazines etc.	8–8.30	Supper/Chat
11 p.m.	Bed	8.30–9.30	Study
		9.30–11	Read/Watch TV/Go to the pub
		11 p.m.	Bed

1 How many study hours (i.e. excluding classes etc) do Bill and Jim have each day?
2 They have each been given an essay on Monday morning to be done by the following Monday.
'I have a week to do the essay.'
How many *study hours* does this mean in each case?
3 Assume that the academic year lasts 40 weeks, and that Bill and Jim do not change their daily routine. By the end of the year, how many study hours will each of the students have put in?

Notice that the point of this exercise is not to say that Bill is studying too little, or that Jim spends too much time in the library. Perhaps Bill is extremely intelligent and does not need to study as long as Jim. Perhaps Jim is not a very efficient student and does not make the best use of the time he spends 'studying'. The point is simply that 'a year's work' or 'a week's work' may mean very different things according to your routine. It is important for you to know how many hours you *can* and *do* spend on study in an average week.

Study hours routine

If you have already made out a personal timetable for unit 1, you should find the information you need here by simply referring back to that unit.

Go through each day of a normal week and write down how many hours you think you have available for private study each day.

At the end of each day write down the *actual* number of hours you spent on private study beside the *possible* hours. (Do not count 'taught periods', i.e. lectures, supervised lab work etc.)

Are there any differences between *actual* and *possible* hours? If there are, make a note to explain why. Is this because of
a)   the amount of work you had to do?
or
b)   the fact that you under-estimated or (more likely!) over-estimated the amount of time? If so, write down new, revised estimate and see if you can keep to it next week.

Going through the 'Study hours routine' should give a more realistic idea of the amount of time that you really have available for private study. Your next job is to establish how you are going to use these hours.

Exercise 5

What is the best use that can be made of private study hours? Obviously some of the time (probably a lot of it) will be taken up with doing *prescribed work* (essays etc). Are there any other useful ways of using private study time? List them.

Discuss your ideas with the other members of the group.

Revision
Did you list 'revision' as one of the uses of private study time? It tends to be pushed into the background, but is very important as we shall see.

Exercise 6

1 Look at this diagram.

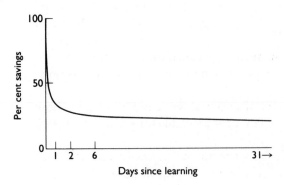

Days since learning

The Ebbinghaus forgetting curve
This curve, which records the results of an experiment by a famous psychologist called Ebbinghaus, shows the rate at which people forget. The original experiment tested memory of nonsense syllables, but has been shown to be valid for a wide range of remembering activities. (Diagram from Deese 1964, after Ebbinghaus 1885)

Suppose we treat the 'savings' in the Ebbinghaus experiment as 'amount remembered'. How much was remembered, roughly,

a) after one day?
b) after two days?
c) after six days?
d) after 31 days?
e) When did most forgetting take place?
f) What would you say is the most interesting information that this diagram gives you about the rate of forgetting?

2 Look at this diagram.

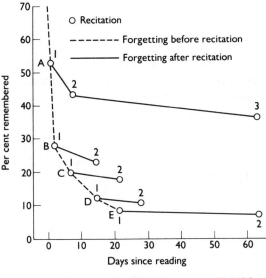

Days since reading

How forgetting is reduced by recitation (i.e. attempting to repeat from memory what one has learnt)
Five groups of children (A, B, C, D, E) were given an article to read. Each group was then tested on the content of the article at different intervals. The students were not allowed to revise the article and were not given the correct results of the tests. The curve therefore shows the effects of simply *trying to remember*. (Diagram adapted from Deese 1964, after Spitzer, 1939)

a) Which group of children remembered most?
b) Which remembered least?

c) What does this diagram show us about the value of *trying to remember* something after we have read it or been taught it?
d) What is the best time for the effort to remember?
e) The diagram tells interesting things also about *the rate of forgetting*. What do you notice when you compare the rate of forgetting for Group A after the first test and after the second test?

There is one consolation for the lazy student – all the students seem to have remembered something!

To summarise what we have learned from the data in the two diagrams, we can say that:
1 As far as detailed material is concerned, about 80% of what is learned will be forgotten unless something is done to prevent this.
2 One obvious way to prevent forgetting is revision. If you cannot revise, even the act of *trying* to remember the material ('recitation') will slow up the forgetting process.
3 Most of the forgetting takes place within 24 hours.
4 Therefore, the sooner the revision/recitation process is done after learning the better.
5 The more frequently the revision/recitation is done, the more slowly the forgetting takes place.
6 Frequent revision is therefore better than leaving all the revision to near the examination. By that time, the task of *re-learning* the material will be much harder.

Revision and memorisation routine

1 Set aside a period every day when you will quickly revise the notes and reading you have done during the day.
2 After every lecture, tutorial, seminar, lab session, or reading session, try to go over in your mind what the main points of the lecture, text etc were.

Remembering
We have just seen that one way of remembering what you have studied or been taught is prompt and frequent revision. You will have noticed, however, that the experiments by Ebbinghaus were based on repeating nonsense syllables. Let us explore this a bit further.

Exercise 7

Read through this list in the order indicated, once, slowly. Then close the book and see how many of the syllables you can say or write down *in the correct order*. (Mark an item wrong if it is out of order.)

1	MED	6	TIR
2	NIZ	7	MAB
3	SIQ	8	KYB
4	QOL	9	GIK
5	NUX	10	JOF

Exercise 8

Do this exercise in the same way as exercise 3.

1	SAT	6	MAT
2	THE	7	THAT
3	FOR	8	ON
4	CAT	9	WHOLE
5	HOUR	10	ONE

Exercise 9

Now do the same with these:

1	THE	6	MAT
2	CAT	7	FOR
3	SAT	8	ONE
4	ON	9	WHOLE
5	THAT	10	HOUR

Exercise 10

Read over this list of numbers (reading from left to right). You have one minute to remember the numbers by reading them slowly in groups of three.

```
2  9  3  3  3  6  4  0  4  3  4  7
5  8  1  2  1  5  1  9  2  2  2  6
```

Now close the book and see how many of the figures you remembered in the correct order.

Exercise 11

Now you can try to do the same exercise again. You have one minute. But this time you must try to look for some *system* in the numbers. Here is a clue: start with the *bottom* line at the left hand side, and try adding 3 to the first number and 4 to the second number.

```
2  9  3  3  3  6  4  0  4  3  4  7
5  8  1  2  1  5  1  9  2  2  2  6
```

Now close the book and see how many of the numbers you can write down *in the correct order*.

One would expect people to do exercise 9 better than 8, and exercise 8 better than exercise 7. Also, if the system has been discovered, exercise 11 is much easier than exercise 10. Why is this? Obviously, because things are easier to remember if they are
a) meaningful
and
b) systematic
Thus exercise 9 is easy because the words are meaningful (unlike exercise 7), and organised in a meaningful way (unlike exercise 8). Exercise 17 is easy once you have recognised the *system*. Organising things into a system means that you have fewer things to remember. It follows therefore that
a) it is very inefficient to try to remember something you don't really understand,
b) one way of making material easy to remember is to organise it in some way. Plans, charts and diagrams can be very helpful in this respect.

Go back to unit 2, exercise 9 (p. 23). Read through the article on 'Malaria' quickly and then look at the outline diagram on p. 184. You will see that the main points have been highlighted, and the material has been organised in a way that should make it easier to remember. One-page outlines of this type of probable examination topics could be an invaluable help in pre-examination revision.

MALARIA — A NEW THREAT

Female ANOPHELES mosquito $\longrightarrow$ MALARIA

FOUGHT BY

1. Breeding places
   - drained or
   - covered with oil /detergent

2. New varieties $\longrightarrow$ females infertile

   BUT many (2600+) varieties.

3. Wire Screens
   Mosquito Netting

ALSO

4. Drugs   e.g. quinine
   other new drugs

   BUT germs becoming resistant

5. Insecticides   e.g. D.D.T.
   BUT mosquitoes becoming resistant

∴ new threat.

Example of the kind of one-page diagram layout which is easier to remember

Exercise 12

1 Quickly read through the article in unit 2 on 'Aspects of the reading process and reading efficiency' (p. 12). Try making a one-page organised summary of it similar to the one above.
2 Take a chapter or a section of any text that you have had to read recently. Make a one-page outline summary of it.

Rote memory

Sometimes, however, we *do* have to remember things in a rote fashion, i.e. the meaning of the words is not much help to us. A medical student, for example, may have to learn a list of names of bones, a history student a list of dates; there are also lists of chemical elements, mathematical formulae etc. The secret here is that we must *make* the items in the list meaningful (since they are not meaningful in themselves) and *relate* them to one another in any way we can. One way of doing this is by using a *mnemonic* (pronounced /ni'monik/). Mnemonics were invented in the times of the ancient Greeks and have been used by students ever since. Here are some examples of how mnemonics work (the second and third examples are from the useful and amusing *Dictionary of Mnemonics* published by Eyre Methuen):

1 By making up a rhyme.
    (To remember the spelling of words like *brief, belief, receive, deceit* etc which are spelled with an *i* and an *e*, and have the sound /i:/.)
        i before *e*
        Except after *c*.
    (There are five exceptions: *weird, seize, counterfeit, weir* and *plebeian*. Perhaps you could think of another mnemonic for the exceptions!)
2 By using the number of letters in a word to represent a number in a mathematical formula.
    (To remember $\sqrt{2} = 1\cdot414$. The mnemonic uses the fact that the pronoun *I* has one letter, while *wish* and *knew* each have four. It also uses rhyme.)
        I wish I knew the root of two.
3 By using the initial letters of the words to be memorised. This is probably the easiest kind of mnemonic for you to make up for yourself. In Biology, to remember the parts of an insect's leg (coxa, trochanter, femur, tibia, tarsus, claw) we have:
    *C*ockroaches *t*ravel *f*ast *t*owards *t*heir *c*hildren.

If there is a list that you have to learn off by heart, or a formula that you keep forgetting, try to make up your own mnemonic. The very act of making it up will help you.

You must remember, though, that you are not likely to pass an examination simply by memorising lists of things. It is more important that what you learn should be *meaningful* to you, and organised in a *systematic* way.

Memorising routine

1 Reduce the amount that you have to learn by concentrating on the main ideas. Don't try to remember everything.
2 Organise your material in a concise way, using diagrams etc when you can.
3 Relate the things that you learn to each other, and also to your own life and thoughts.
4 Don't waste your time trying to remember what you don't understand.
5 If there is a list you have to learn off by heart, or two things that you keep confusing, try to associate them in some meaningful way, e.g. by making up a mnemonic.

Before the examination

We have already seen above that there is research which shows that many students claim that they study long hours, but do not seem to get the rewards for the hours they put in. Since all students who get into a college or university should be of above average intelligence, lack of intelligence cannot explain all of these cases. Malleson, whose research we have already referred to, found that there were four kinds of student who spent a lot of time on 'study', to very little effect.

Have you any suggestions of what these students might do to help themselves? (There is a longer discussion of this topic in Allen (1966); the quotations are all from Malleson (1961) as quoted by Allen.)

Exercise 13

1 *Student A has poor study habits and is generally disorganised.* 'For a few days he does nothing at all; then, particularly if he is to be required to hand in an essay, he makes a great rush at it, reading hurriedly and with great confusion. His written work tends to be untidy and his notes such that he never has the material ready for the revision he intends to do.'
2 *Student B is obsessed with 'rituals', i.e. things he feels he must do before he can start studying.* 'Here the student finds it extremely difficult to get started on his studying. Obsessionally he makes

out elaborate timetables and plans but he never really manages to begin. He collects textbooks together, arranges pads of loose-leaf paper in neat piles, he sharpens pencils, and collects rubbers, but then somehow he gets ensnared deeper and deeper in the complication of the small-type footnotes of his textbooks. An enormous amount of time may actually be involved in the whole process – he is not a slacker – but very little actual work is accomplished.'

3 *Student C has problems with remembering what he has studied.* Allen (1966) suggests that there are really two kinds of student here:

   a) the ones who have personal problems which are distracting them from their studies.

   b) the ones who are not really learning the material at all either because they cannot understand it or because they are not interested in it.

4 *Student D knows the material but cannot produce it under pressure in a seminar or examination situation.* This student is terrified of making mistakes or making a fool of himself, so he never says anything. In an examination, he panics and cannot get his answers down.

Notice that we have been discussing only students who work hard. There are other students who do not work because they are not motivated, or because they are easily distracted etc.

Exercise 14

You might find it useful to have a class discussion on the basis of what you have written for exercise 13. If you have any study problems which are of a personal nature, you could perhaps discuss them privately with your tutor. You will probably discover, however, that problems which you thought were yours alone actually affect other students too. Many of the problems are rooted in fear – if you look at them rationally and discuss them with others, they will probably become much less serious.

Revision period routine

1 Do you know the *time*, *date* and *place* of the examination? Note down the details.

2 Check them again.

3 For each examination, do you know

   a) the length of the examination?

   b) the number of questions on the paper?

   c) how the paper is organised?

d) how many questions you have to do?

e) the nature of the questions (e.g. essay, multiple-choice, etc)?

4 Have you decided how long you are going to allow yourself for each question?

5 Have you made a list of the questions which you expect to be asked (or some of them, at least)?

6 Have you prepared a one-page organised summary for each question you expect to be asked?

7 If the answer to 5 is 'No', will you allow time for that in your revision period?

8 Have you prepared a revision timetable in terms of *study hours per day*?

9 How many study hours per week have you allowed yourself? (If the answer is more than 50 hours, including classes etc that you have to attend, think again. You may be overburdening yourself.)

10 Have you set aside some time for relaxation? (You should do so.)

11 Have you arranged that the day before the examination involves some work, but not too much?

12 Does your revision plan involve many late nights of study? (Your answers to 11 and 12 should be 'Yes' and 'No' respectively. Remember that you will have to think and react quickly during the examination. You cannot do that if you are fatigued.)

During the examination

Day of the examination routine

1 Get up in plenty of time.

2 Make sure that any equipment you need (calculators etc.) is
a) in working order
b) where you cannot possibly leave it behind in a last-minute rush.

3 There should be no last-minute rush! Get to the examination hall in plenty of time. You will be at a great psychological disadvantage if you are late, or even just in time.

4 Check through the instructions carefully. There may have been changes since the last examination.

5 Be sure about the number of questions you have to do.

6 Tick the questions you intend to do. Decide when you ought to end each question. Note the time down beside the question.

7   Start with the easiest question. If it is an essay-type question, jot down any ideas at all in any order that they come to you. This will prevent you from 'drying up'. Organise your notes roughly. Spend some time on this, but not too much, e.g. for a one-hour answer, ten minutes might be the maximum time on preparation.

8   Do each of the questions in turn ending with the one you know least about.

9   Watch your time. Make sure that you write something on each question. If you do run out of time, you can answer the question (or part of it) in note form.

10 Leave a few minutes at the end for checking over the paper. Be careful about the legibility of your handwriting – if necessary write out illegible words and phrases again.

References

Clifford Allen (1966)   *Passing Examinations* (Revised edition, Pan Books, London)

James Deese (1964)   *Principles of Psychology* (Allyn & Bacon, Boston)

H. Ebbinghaus (1885; English trans. 1913)   *Memory* Columbia University Coll. Educ. Reprints, No. 3, (Teachers' College, Columbia University, New York)

N. Malleson (1961)   'Academic study and mental health', *Student Mental Health* (London)

H. F. Spitzer (1939)   'Studies in retention', *Journal of Educational Psychology*, Vol. 30, (1939), pp. 641–56

Appendix

Unit 1

Key to the questionnaires (answers given by the average successful student)

1 *College work*

1 Yes	2 Yes	3 Yes	4 No	5 No	6 No
7 Yes	8 Yes	9 Yes	10 Yes	11 No	12 Yes

2 *Private study*
Yes to all questions.

3 *General way of life*
Yes to all questions

Unit 2

Exercise 3

Answer

1 'Italian migration to Britain'
Among other points the article covers:
  a) the rate of Italian migration to Britain.
  b) which parts of Italy migrants came from.
  c) the jobs they do in Britain.
  d) how far they have integrated into British society.
  e) the parts of Britain that they have settled in.

2 'Water in Kuwait'
Among other points the article covers:
  a) the great shortage of water in Kuwait.
  b) the programme for using salt sea water.
  c) other sources of water supply.
  d) the discouragement of wasteful use of water.
  e) the possibility of water-rationing.

3 'Life in India behind the veil' (Text title: 'Purdah: life behind the veil')
  a) Social customs for women in a small village in India.
  b) Recent changes in these social customs.

4 'First colony in space' (Text title: 'The next frontier')
  a) describes an imaginary journey to a space colony in the year AD 2026.
  b) discusses how feasible (possible) such a colony is.
  c) describes how people will live and the technology involved.

5 'Solar Energy, the Ultimate Powerhouse'
   Among other things, the article
   a) discusses the energy crisis.
   b) describes techniques for using the power of the sun.
   c) discusses which techniques are currently available and which are
      still experimental.
   d) discusses the expense involved in fitting solar energy units, and
      how much money they save.

Exercise 11

Answers
1 draining; covering with oil or detergent.
2 getting different varieties to mate (females infertile)
3 using screens and netting; drugs (e.g. quinine); insecticides(e.g. DDT)
4 drugs; insecticides.

Exercise 16

Answers
2 a) true
2 b) false
2 c) true
2 d) false
2 e) false

Exercise 17

Answers
2 a) false
2 b) false
2 c) true
2 d) false
2 e) true

Reading speed table

Time	Exercise 11 533 words	Exercise 14 580 words	Exercises 8,17 615 words	Exercise 16 720 words	Exercise 10 760 words	Exercise 15 880 words
1.00	533	580	*	*	*	*
10	456	495	525	*	*	*
20	400	436	462	541	577	*
30	355	386	410	480	507	586
40	321	349	370	434	458	530
50	291	317	336	393	415	480
2.00	266	290	308	360	380	440
10	246	267	283	331	350	406
20	229	249	264	309	326	378
30	213	232	246	288	304	352
40	200	218	231	271	286	331
50	188	205	217	254	269	310
3.00	178	193	205	240	253	293
10	168	183	194	227	240	278
20	160	174	185	216	228	264
30	152	166	176	206	217	251
40	146	158	168	197	208	240
50	139	151	161	188	198	230
4.00	133	145	154	180	190	220
10	128	139	147	173	182	211
20	123	134	142	166	176	203
30	118	129	137	160	169	196
40	114	124	132	155	163	189
50	110	120	127	149	157	182
5.00	106	116	123	144	152	176
10	103	112	119	139	147	170
20	100	109	115	135	143	165
30	97	105	112	131	138	160
40	94	102	109	127	134	155
50	91	99	105	123	130	151
6.00	89	97	103	120	127	147
10	86	94	100	117	123	143
20	84	92	97	114	120	139
30	82	89	95	111	116	135
40	80	87	92	108	114	132
50	*	85	90	105	111	129
7.00	*	83	88	103	109	126
10	*	81	86	100	106	123
20	*	*	84	98	104	120
30	*	*	82	96	101	117
40	*	*	80	94	99	114
50	*	*	*	92	97	112
8.00	*	*	*	90	95	110
10	*	*	*	88	93	108
20	*	*	*	86	91	106
30	*	*	*	84	89	104
40	*	*	*	83	87	101
50	*	*	*	82	86	100
9.00				80	84	98
10				*	83	96
20				*	81	94
30				*	80	93
40				*	*	91
50				*	*	90
10.00					*	88
10					*	87
20					*	85
30					*	84
40					*	83
50					*	81
11.00					*	80

Unit 3

Exercise 12

Materials for recording and storing information

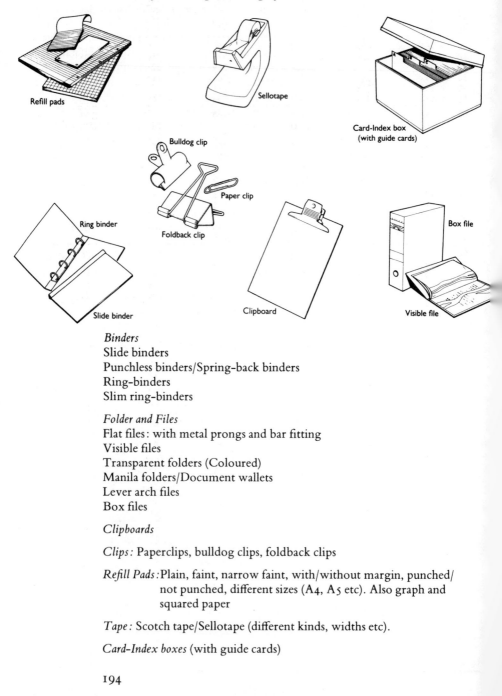

Binders
Slide binders
Punchless binders/Spring-back binders
Ring-binders
Slim ring-binders

Folder and Files
Flat files: with metal prongs and bar fitting
Visible files
Transparent folders (Coloured)
Manila folders/Document wallets
Lever arch files
Box files

Clipboards

Clips: Paperclips, bulldog clips, foldback clips

Refill Pads: Plain, faint, narrow faint, with/without margin, punched/
not punched, different sizes (A4, A5 etc). Also graph and
squared paper

Tape: Scotch tape/Sellotape (different kinds, widths etc).

Card-Index boxes (with guide cards)

194

Volcanoes

Today I am going to talk to you about volcanoes. In the first part of my lecture I am going to discuss what volcanoes are and how they are caused. Then I shall mention some examples of famous volcanoes and I'd like you to note the details about them as well.

First of all, what *are* volcanoes? Everyone I think has a mental picture of a volcano – in appearance it looks like a cone-shaped mountain. But the top of the cone is rather flat and hollow. This is the crater, which is, as it were, the mouth of the volcano. The volcano is formed by molten rock coming up from below the earth's crust; by *molten* rock we mean rock which is so hot that it runs like liquid. This rock is called LAVA.

Imagine a sort of pipe coming up from deep down in the earth's surface, passing through the rocks of the earth's crust and coming up to the crater. The lava forces its way up this pipe and overflows to form the sides of the volcano. The volcanic mountain is therefore formed from the lava and ashes pushed up from below the earth's surface.

Volcanoes are therefore found in areas where the earth's surface is for some reason weak, and cannot resist the pressure of the molten lava.

I am now going to mention some famous volcanic eruptions or explosions that you should know about. The greatest volcanic eruption of recent years was when KRAKATOA, an island in Indonesia, was almost completely blown up. The noise of the explosion was heard 3,000 miles away.

Volcanoes can be formed very quickly. In PARÍCUTIN in Mexico a volcanic mountain 1,000 feet high and 3,000 feet across was formed from level ground in four months.

Volcanoes can be very desctructive too. In May 1902 a volcano called MONT PELÉE on the island of MARTINIQUE erupted, killing about 40,000.

One of the most famous volcanic eruptions of ancient times was the famous eruption of Mount VESUVIUS near Naples in 79 AD. Some neighbouring towns were buried under huge amounts of ash. The ash preserved the bodies of many of the victims which can still be seen today.

Model notes

What are volcanoes?

CRATER

SIDES FORMED FROM LAVA + ASH

LAVA 'PIPE'

ROCKS OF EARTH'S CRUST

Famous Volcanoes

1. KRAKATOA (Indonesia)   Noise heard 3000 miles away

2. PARÍCUTIN (Mexico)   1000 ft. high.
   3000 ft. across
   Formed in 4 months

3. MONT PELÉE (Martinique)   Killed 40,000 people

4. VESUVIUS (Naples)   79 A.D.

   Ash preserved bodies of victims.

1 (*Politics*)
When a party is elected to Parliament in Britain it may not stay in
power for more than five years without calling an election. But –
now this is an important point – the Prime Minister may 'go to the
country', that's to say call an election *at any time* before the five years
are up. This is important because it gives the Prime Minister in
Britain a lot of power – he can choose the best time to have an
election for his own party. In many other countries the timing of an
election is fixed – it must take place on a certain date every four years,
or whatever, and this means that in these countries the President or
Prime Minister cannot choose the most convenient time for himself,
the way a British Prime Minister can.

2 (*Medicine*)
One of the most dramatic examples of the effect of advances in
medical knowledge is the building of the Panama Canal. In 1881
work was started on this canal under the supervision of De Lesseps,
the Frenchman who built the Suez canal. The project had to be
abandoned after mosquito-borne diseases of yellow fever and malaria
had claimed 16,000 victims among the workers. At the beginning of
this century, the area was made healthy by spraying the breeding
waters of the mosquitoes with petroleum. Work was able to be
started again and the canal was finished in 1914.

3 (*Sport*)
By the way, since we have mentioned the Olympic Games, you may
be interested to know the following curious fact about the ancient
Olympic Games as compared to the Modern Olympics. The ancient
games were held every four years *without interruption* for over 1,000
years. The modern games have already been cancelled three times (in
1916, 1940 and 1944) because of world wars.

4 (*Zoology*)
Although it is not strictly speaking relevant to our topic, perhaps I
might say something about sharks since they are in the news quite a
lot these days. Sharks have got a very bad reputation and probably
most people think that all sharks are killers. This is not the case. In
fact, the largest sharks of all (I mean the Whale Shark and the Basking
Shark) are usually harmless to man.

5 (*Literature*)
We may note in passing that, although Dr Johnson's friend and
biographer (Boswell) was a Scotsman, Johnson despised, or pretended
to despise, Scotsmen in general. He once said that the best thing a
Scotsman ever saw was the high road to England. In his famous
dictionary, Johnson defined oats as 'a grain which in England is
generally given to horses, but in Scotland supports the people'. He
did not condemn all Scotsmen, however. Once he commented on a
distinguished nobleman who had been born in Scotland but educated
in England, saying that much could be made of a Scotsman – *if he was
caught young.*

6 (*Geography: American Indians*)
The first important point to note about the American Indians is that,

in spite of their name, they are in no way related to the peoples of India. This confusion arose, as you probably know, because of a mistake on the part of Christopher Columbus. When he landed in America he thought that he had in fact discovered India. This mistake has been perpetrated, that is kept alive, ever since by the name he gave them. If they are related to any Asian group it is to the Mongols of Northern Asia. Many experts believe that the ancestors of the present American Indians emigrated from Northern Asia across the Bering Strait between 10,000 and 20,000 years ago.

7 (*Science: methods of scientific discovery*)
A good illustration of how scientific discoveries may be made accidentally is the discovery of penicillin. Alexander Fleming was a bacteriologist who for fifteen years had tried to solve the problem of how to get rid of the disease-carrying germs or microbes in the human body without causing any dangerous side-effects. Fleming was an untidy worker and often had innumerable small dishes containing microbes all around his laboratory. One day, one of the dishes was contaminated with a mould, due to the window having been left open. Fleming noticed that the mould had killed off the microbes, and it was from similar moulds that the miracle drug penicillin was finally developed. Of course, only a brilliant scientist like Fleming would have been able to take advantage of this stroke of luck, but the fact remains that the solution to his problem was given to him, literally, on a plate.

8 (*Psychology: memory*)
What I want to emphasise to you is this: that people remember things which make sense to them or which they can connect with something they already know. Students who try to memorise what they cannot understand are almost certainly wasting their time.

Exercise 16

The strengths of British trade unions

In this talk I would like to deal with the sources of the strength of the trade union movement in Britain.

Trade unions in Britain are generally believed nowadays to be in a position of great political strength. What is this strength based on? I am going to suggest that it is based on three things: political power, economic power and the protection of the law.

Well, firstly, through their influence on the Labour Party they have *political* power. Their influence over the Labour Party is demonstrated by the following three facts. One is that about one-third of the Labour Party MPs are sponsored by trade unions. This means that a trade union who sponsors a successful candidate will, among other things, provide the bulk of his expenses and in some cases even pay him an allowance.

The second relevant fact is that the unions are the main source of finance for the Labour Party. In 1966, the Party received seven times as much in affiliation fees (that's to say, roughly, membership fees) from the trade unions as from the CONSTITUENCY associations.

The third fact is that the unions are in a position to dominate decisions at the Labour Party Conference for they control $5\frac{1}{2}$ million votes as against 800,000 from the constituencies. Through their domination of the Party Conference they are able to influence both the policy and the administration of the Party.

So much for the unions' *political power*.

Secondly, of course, the trade unions have *economic power*, in that they can take industrial action. There has been no general strike in Britain since 1926, but certain unions are in a position to paralyse key industries and thus bring great pressure to bear on the government.

Thirdly, the unions have some degree of *legal protection*. This takes two forms. The first one is the protection of the labour laws. By this we are referring to the Trade Disputes Acts of 1906 and 1965. The Act of 1906 states that 'no action against a trade . . . in respect of any tort (that is, roughly, any offence) alleged to have been committed . . . shall be entertained by any court'. This puts the unions, in a sense, outside the law.

Another kind of legal immunity is that trade unions are excluded from MONOPOLY legislation. If a manufacturerer uses his total control over certain goods or services to push up prices, that is an offence. But it is not an offence for unions to use their monopoly over the work-force to push up wages, and, consequently prices.

So we therefore have three sources of strength for the unions: political power through their influence on the Labour Party; economic power based on their right to strike; and legal protection.

Exercise 17

The weaknesses of British trade unions

In the last talk, we discussed the strengths of the trade union movement in Britain. But it is generally agreed that this strength has not been realised. Why is this so? For the answer we shall have to look at the *weaknesses* of the trade union movement. I think that there are three sources of weakness: disunity, incompetence and unpopularity.

The first weakness is *disunity*. The Trades Union Congress is not a governing body. It can take decisions but it cannot enforce them on all the members. For example, the craft unions, that is the unions of skilled workers, do not always agree with each other. The craft unions, in turn, wish to preserve their differentials against the unskilled or semi-skilled members of the general unions. Again, established unions are opposed to the development of new unions, and so on. Another source of disunity is the power of the shop stewards who may oppose the authority of the central union administration. Also unofficial leaders of the workers in a certain factory may emerge.

A second weakness may be put under the heading of *incompetence*: The trade union movement is not expanding. Only 40% of the total working population belong to trade unions: three reasons can be advanced for this state of affairs: *apathy* (very few members take an active interest in their union affairs); secondly, *lack of finance* (few unions have the funds to sustain a long strike, although the fact that the families or dependents of strikers may get social security benefits helps to counter-balance this); and thirdly, the quality of union *leadership*.

A third weakness is that trade unions are *unpopular*. Opinion polls in the 1960s have shown a decline in public esteem. People are tending more and more to blame the unions for the economic ills of the country. Ordinary people often find the DEMARCATION disputes over who does what job silly and pointless, although the consequences may be serious enough for the workers involved in the disputes. There is also sometimes resentment over the way that union members treat the individual worker who, for example, refuses to join in a strike and so on. Strikes may also make unions unpopular. They are intended to hurt the interests of the employers. But in the case of, say, a transport strike it is often other workers who are directly penalised.

The impact of trade unions on political life is therefore lessened by the fact that they are often disunited, and sometimes seem to be incompetent and appear unpopular.

(For the material presented in exercises 16 and 17 I am indebted to C. J. Wates and S. T. Miller: *A Visual Approach to British and American Government*, Longman 1973.)

Exercise 21

Model notes

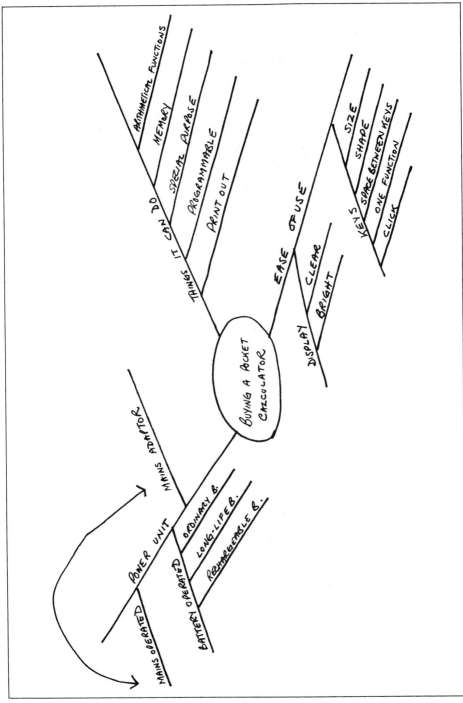

Exercise 22

Model notes

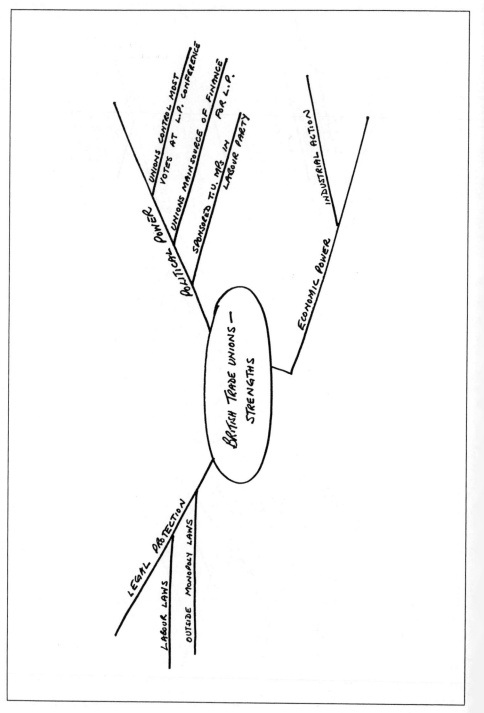

Exercise 23

Model notes

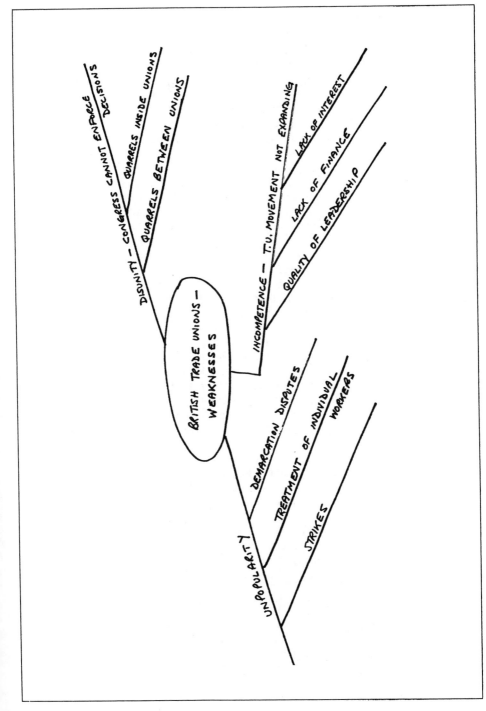

Solving problems

Today I am going to talk about some thoughts that psychologists have had on how people go about solving problems.

The first point I want to make is that there is no *one* way of solving *all* problems. If you think about it you will realise the obvious fact that there are many different kinds of problems which have to be solved in different ways. Let us take two very different examples.

A student is sitting in his study, trying to solve a problem in Mathematics. After an hour, still unsuccessful, he gives up and goes to bed. The following morning he wakes up and wanders into the study. Suddenly, the solution comes to him.

Now for a very different kind of problem. In the Shakespeare play *Hamlet*, young Hamlet, Prince of Denmark, discovers that his father has been murdered by his uncle. The evidence is based on the appearance of his father's ghost, urging him to revenge his death by killing his uncle. Should he accept the ghost's evidence, and kill his uncle? This is obviously a very different kind of problem. Such moral or emotional problems might have no real solution, or at any rate no solution that everyone might agree on.

There are many other different types of problems apart from these two. In this talk, I would like to talk about the first kind of problem: the kind that the student of Mathematics was involved with.

The solution to that kind of problem is sometimes called an 'A-ha' solution, because the solution comes suddenly, out of nowhere as it were, and in English people sometimes say 'A-ha' when a good idea comes to them like that. Another, less amusing, name for it is insight. For a long time the student seems to get nowhere, and then there is a sudden flash of insight and the solution appears.

A classic example of insight is the case of the French mathematician POINCARÉ. For fifteen days Poincaré struggled with a mathematical problem and had no success. Then one evening he took black coffee before going to bed (which was not his usual custom). As he lay in bed, he couldn't sleep, and all sorts of ideas came to him. By morning he had solved the problem which had baffled him for over a fortnight.

What do psychologists have to say about this process of problem solving?

A very good and helpful description of the solving process has been made by POLYA, a teacher of Mathematics. Remember that Polya is thinking of insight problems, and in particular, mathematics problems: but his ideas should apply in all sorts of areas.

Polya's description has four stages. They are:

Stage one: *Understanding the problem*: At this stage, the student gathers all the information he needs and asks himself two questions:
The first question is:
What is the unknown? What is my *goal*? In other words, what do I want to find out?

The second question is:
>What are the data and conditions? What is *given*? In other words:
>What do I already know?

Stage two: *Devising a plan*: Here the student makes use of his past experience to decide on the method of solution. At this stage he asks himself three questions:

a) Do I know a problem similar to this one?

b) Can I restate the *goal* in a different way that will make it easier for me to use my past experience? Polya calls restating the goal 'working backwards'.

c) Can I restate what is *given* in a way that relates to my past experience? Polya calls restating what is given as 'working forward'. The student stays at stage two until he has the flash of insight. If necessary he can put the problem to one side for a while and then come back to it. Eventually he will see how the problem can be done.

Stage three: *Carrying out the plan*: The student carries out the plan of solution, checking each step.

Stage four: *Looking back*: The student checks his answer in some way, perhaps by using another method, or whatever. Having done that, he makes it part of his experience by asking himself: 'Can I use this result or method for other problems'?

I will repeat again that not all problems are like the mathematics problems that Polya is thinking about. Not every problem is solvable, and some may even have no satisfactory solution. Nevertheless, it is probably a good idea to do what Polya has done. That is, when you are successful in solving a problem, analyse how you have done it, and remember your method for the next time.

(The student will find a fuller account of Polya's work, and that of other writers in this area, in Richard E. Mayer: *Thinking and Problem Solving: An Introduction to Human Cognition and Learning*: Scott Foresman, Glenview, Illinois, 1977.)

Model notes

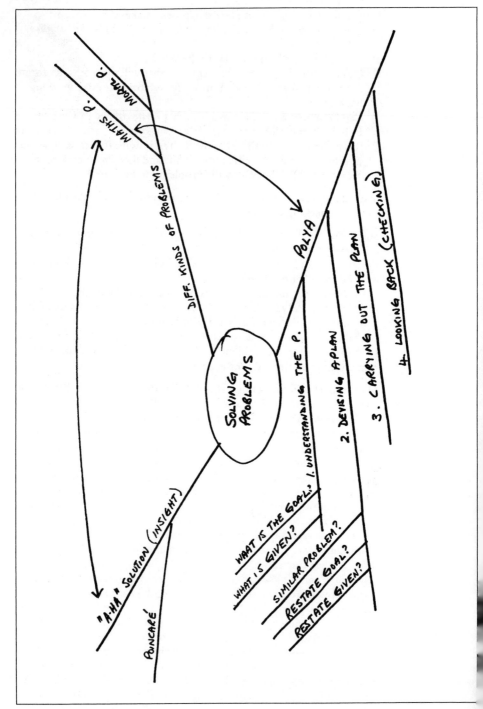

Communication

Today we are going to discuss communication. Now, we are going to concentrate on the means of communication, and we are going to consider them in four general categories. These categories are: speech, writing, printing and electronic communication. I will take each of them in turn and discuss them briefly.

The oldest of these forms of communication is undoubtedly speech. It is believed that speech originated perhaps one million years ago, possibly by imitation of natural sounds. Certainly there are many such words as *bang*, or *buzz* which are imitative in function.

The next big step forward in communication was the invention of writing. It had two major advantages over speech. Firstly, the speaker himself did not have to be present in order to communicate. And secondly, the knowledge of one generation could be accumulated and passed on to the next.

Now, the first kind of writing was picture writing, where the scribe drew a picture of what he wanted to represent. These can be seen in the ancient Egyptian HIEROGLYPHICS, or in some modern Chinese IDEOGRAPHS. Having to draw everything you want to communicate, is of course, very limiting. Many of these drawings took on other meanings, and some cases came to represent sounds. The use of symbols to represent sounds was a great breakthrough. It led to the use of SYLLABARIES – that is systems where each symbol stood for a syllable; vowels were not indicated. Later came the invention of the alphabet: that is to say the representation of each sound by a different symbol. In spite of its advantage writing was, and is, a slow and cumbersome process and so the ability to write remained the privilege of a few until the invention of printing. This originated in China, where blocks of wood were carved into the shape of letters covered in ink, and pressed onto paper. The Arabs brought the secret of printing to Europe around the tenth century. But it was not until the sixteenth century that European printers started to use the much more useful metal type. They also adapted the wine-press used for crushing grapes, and used it for pressing their new metal type onto paper. So the number of books vastly multiplied with tremendous consequences for the development of science and indeed all aspects of human culture.

The most recent development has been the use of electronic means of communication. These can be subdivided into those which require a wire or cable connection for transferring messages (such as the telephone) and those which do not (such as radio and television). The pioneer in this area was Samuel B. MORSE who devised a method of sending messages by using short and long signals (dots and dashes). This system is still known today as the Morse Code. The invention of the telephone made the learning of a special code unnecessary: people could speak to one another quite naturally. The invention of wireless-radio communication by MARCONI in 1896 meant that messages could be sent over long distances without the necessity of using wires or cables, and the first transatlantic wireless message was made in December 1901.

Work started on the development of television in the nineteen-twenties, and the BBC made their first regular transmissions in 1929. But it is only in the last twenty years or so that television has become as popular as radio in many countries.

Exercise 25

Model notes

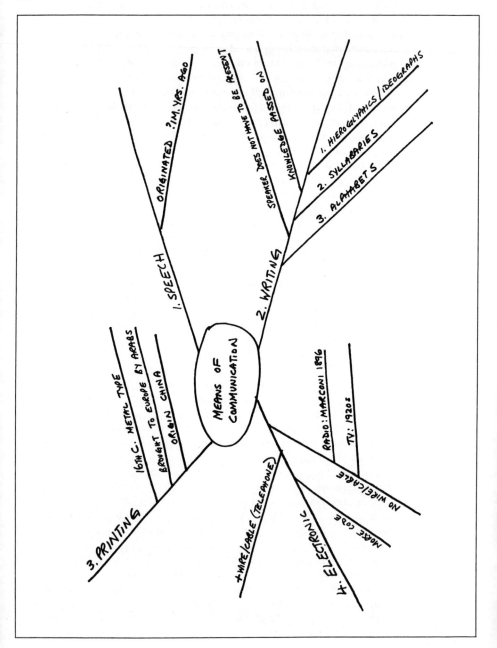

Exercise 26

How to present a seminar paper

In this talk, I am going to give some advice on how to present a seminar paper.

At one time, most university teaching took the form of giving formal lectures. Nowadays, many university teachers try to involve their students more actively in the learning process. One of the ways in which this is done is by conducting seminars. In a seminar, what usually happens is this. One student is chosen to give his ideas on a certain topic. These ideas are then discussed by the other students (the *participants*) in the seminar.

What I'd like to discuss with you today is the techniques of presenting a paper at a seminar. As you know, there are two main stages involved in this. One is the *preparation stage* which involves researching and writing up a topic. The other stage is the *presentation stage* when you actually present the paper to your audience. It is this second stage that I am concerned with now.

Let us therefore imagine that you have been asked to lead off a seminar discussion and that you have done all the necessary preparation. In other words you have done your research and you have written it up. How are you going to present it?

There are two ways in which this can be done.

The first method is to circulate copies of the paper in advance to all the participants. This gives them time to read it before the seminar, so that they can come already prepared with their own ideas about what you have written. The second method is where there is no time for previous circulation, or there is some other reason why the paper cannot be circulated. In that case, of course, the paper will have to read aloud to the group, who will probably make their own notes on it while they are listening.

In this talk, I am going to concentrate on the first method, where the paper is circulated in advance, as this is the most efficient way of conducting a seminar; but most of what I am going to say also applies to the second method; and indeed may be useful to remember any time you have to speak in public.

You will probably be expected to introduce your paper even if it has been circulated beforehand. There are two good reasons for this. One is that the participants may have read the paper but forgotten some of the main points. The second reason is that some of the participants may not in fact have had time to read your paper, although they may have glanced through it quickly. They will therefore not be in a position to comment on it, unless they get some idea of what it is all about.

When you are introducing your paper, what you must *not* do is simply read the whole paper aloud. This is because:

Firstly, if the paper is a fairly long one, there may *not be enough time for discussion*. From your point of view, the discussion is the most important thing. It is very helpful for you if other people criticise your work: in that way you can improve it.

Secondly, a lot of information can be understood when one is reading. It is not so easy to pick up detailed information when one is listening. In other words, there *may be lack of comprehension or understanding*.

Thirdly, it can be very *boring* listening to something being read aloud. Anyway some of your audience may have read your paper carefully and will not thank you for having to go through all of it again.

Therefore, what you must do is follow the following nine points:

1 *Decide on a time limit* for your talk. Tell your audience what it is. Stick to your time limit. This is very important.

2 *Write out your spoken presentation* in the way that you intend to say it. This means that you must do some of the work of writing the paper again, in a sense. You may think that this is a waste of time, but it isn't. If a speaker tries to make a summary of his paper while he is standing in front of his audience, the results are usually disastrous.

3 *Concentrate only on the main points*. Ignore details. Hammer home the essence of your argument. If necessary, find ways of making your basic points so that your audience will be clear about what they are.

4 *Try to make your spoken presentation lively and interesting*. This doesn't necessarily mean telling jokes and anecdotes. But if you *can* think of interesting or amusing examples to illustrate your argument, use them.

5 If you are not used to speaking in public, *write out everything you have to say*, including examples, etc. Rehearse what you are going to say until you are word perfect.

6 When you know exactly what you are going to say, *reduce it to outline notes*. Rehearse your talk again, this time from the outline notes. Make sure you can find your way easily from the outline notes to the full notes, in case you forget something.

7 At the seminar, *speak from the outline notes*. But bring both sets of notes and your original paper to the meeting. Knowing that you have a full set of notes available will be good for your self-confidence.

8 *Look at your audience while you are speaking*. The technique to use is this. First read the appropriate parts of your notes silently (if you are using outline notes, this won't take you long). Then look up at your audience and say what you have to say. Never speak while you are still reading. While you are looking at your audience, try to judge what they are thinking. Are they following you? You will never make contact with your audience if your eyes are fixed on the paper in front of you.

9 *Make a strong ending*. One good way of doing this is to repeat your main points briefly and invite questions or comments.

Perhaps I can sum up by saying this. Remember that listening is very different from reading. Something that is going to be listened to has therefore got to be prepared in a different way from something that is intended to be read.

Exercise 26

Model notes

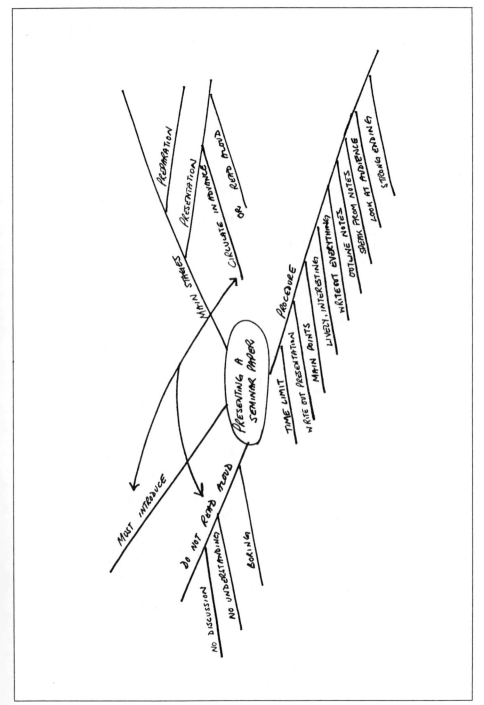

Marriage customs

Today we are going to look at the social custom of *marriage* from a sociological point of view. All societies make provisions for who may mate with whom. The *benefits* of the social recognition of marriage for children are obvious. It gives them an identity, membership of a socially recognised group and some indication of who must support them and their mother.

Now almost all societies have marriage, but there are wide variations in marriage systems. I will give three of the important areas of variation, and some details of each area. The three areas I shall deal with are: firstly, the number of mates each marriage partner may have; secondly, the locality of the marriage (that is, where do the newly married partners set up home?); and thirdly, what arrangements there are for the transfer of wealth after the marriage. Let me deal with each of these in turn.

First, how many mates? In *existing* human societies there are three possibilities. Most societies recognise POLYGYNY, or the right of a man to take more than one wife. In a few societies (not in Africa) there is POLYANDRY, in which a woman is married to two or more men at the same time. Finally, especially in Europe and societies of European origin, there is MONOGAMY. Monogamy limits one man to one wife and vice-versa.

The second area of variation is, as we have said, the locality of the marriage. Here there seem to be three possibilities: at the husband's home, at the wife's home, or in some new place. The old term for the arrangement when a wife moves to her husband's family's household is a PATRILOCAL marriage; a more modern term is VIRILOCAL. The opposite, when the man moves, is termed MATRILOCAL or UXORILOCAL marriage. The third possibility when they set up a new household somewhere else is called NEOLOCAL marriage.

The last area of variation is transfer of wealth on marriage. Here, once more, we seem to have three possibilities. Firstly we have BRIDEWEALTH. In this system wealth is transferred by the husband or his relatives to the bride's family.

This, of course, is the system familiar in Africa. We should remember that the bridewealth may take the form of the husband's labour services to his father-in-law rather than giving cattle or money. In some other societies the opposite system prevails and the wife brings with her a portion or DOWRY in the form of money or other wealth such as land. This was the system of, for example, traditional European societies, and is still practised in the Irish countryside. The third possibility is for the transfer of wealth to take the form of gifts to help the young couple set up the new household. This system is associated with the neolocal type of marriage. In England, these gifts are called wedding-presents. The near kin (that is, the near relatives) of both bride and groom contribute and so do friends, neighbours and workmates. The presents customarily take the form of useful household goods, such as saucepans, tea sets or blankets.

(Adapted from J. E. Goldthorpe: *An Introduction to Sociology*, Cambridge University Press, 2nd edition 1974.)

Exercise 29

Model notes

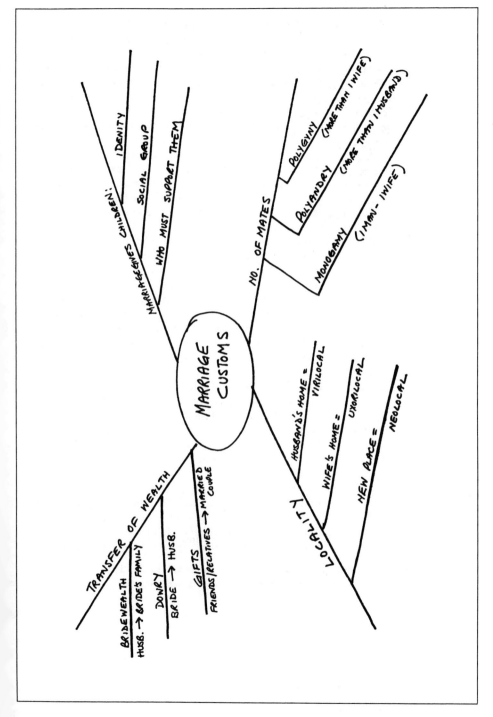

Computers

We have been discussing how a computer works. Now let us turn to another topic: what are the uses of the computer? Many laymen have an exaggerated picture of what computers are capable of. Sometimes computers are called 'electronic brains' and this is confusing, because no computer so far built can compete with the human brain in all respects.

Let us take a look at the applications of computers in commerce and industry. Today, I shall discuss three of the main areas, and I shall give some examples of each. I think you should note the examples, but don't bother too much about the details of each example.

Firstly, clerical work. Computers are very good for handling repetitive clerical work efficiently. We can take two examples of this. The first is the widespread use of computers in handling PAYROLLS, that is, paying employees. Details about each employee (his salary, his tax-code etc) are fed into the computer. The computer makes the necessary calculation and prints out a pay slip.

Another example of the same sort of process has been the use of computers by banks to provide up-to-date records of clients' accounts.

Secondly, we have the use of computers in information systems. The most successful use of these is perhaps the use of computers by airlines to control seat reservation and provide information about flights. British Airways BOADICEA system has 200 terminals in 70 different countries. The main computer store for BOADICEA has a constant record of the details of every flight, including the number of seats available and the names of passengers who have already booked.

Thirdly the computer as an aid to design planning. My first example has to do with predicting *the cost* of a design if one were planning to build a road. One could take a series of photographs of the area; from these, the amount of rise and fall of the landscape can be analysed to within a few inches. This information can be fed into a computer, along with details about what different areas would cost to buy etc. From all this, the computer can be programmed to work out the cheapest route between two points.

My second example has to do with predicting *faults in a design*. It is possible to produce by computer methods pictures of what the road will look like at one metre intervals. It is possible to film each of these as a separate frame, and film them in sequence. In this way, one can spot design faults before the actual construction of the road ever begins.

(Note: for the information in this paragraph I am indebted to Nigel Hawkes: *The Computer Revolution*, Thames & Hudson 1971.)

Exercise 30

Model notes

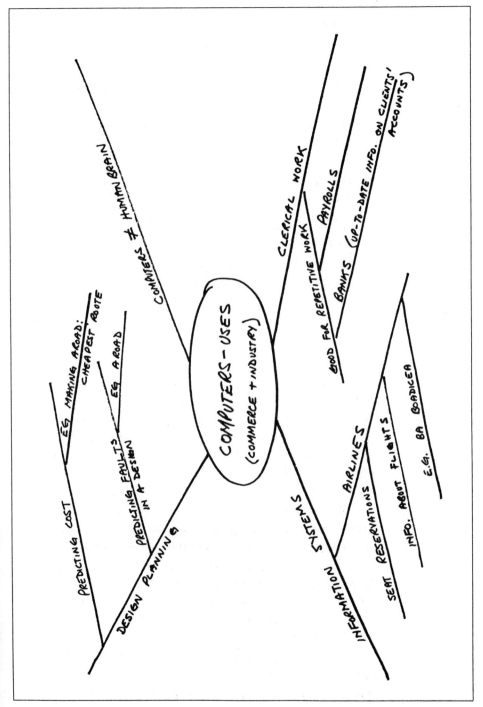

Unit 7

Exercise 4

Correct version

Bibliography

Elliott, Philip (1972)   The Sociology of the Professions.
Macmillan, London

Gerstl, J.E. and Hutton, S.P. (1966)   Engineers: the
Anatomy of a Profession.   Tavistock Publications,
London

Halsey, A.H. and Trow, M. (1971)   The British Academics.
Faber, London

Jackson, J.A. (ed.) (1970)   Professions and
Professionalism. Cambridge University Press, Cambridge

Zander, M. (1968)   Lawyers and the Public Interest.
Weidenfeld & Nicolson, London

Exercise 7

Correct version
(*Note*: there is no one way of writing an essay. There may be other possibilities which are equally correct.)

Tourism is one of the great growth industries of
the last few decades. In most countries there are
official organisations to encourage tourists; and
some countries even have Ministries of Tourism,
so important is this activity.

There are two main arguments for tourism. The
first, and most obvious one, is the economic benefits
which come to the host country. It is usually
people from better-off countries that can afford
to travel, and they bring with them much-needed
'hard currency'. The second argument is that
tourism increases 'international understanding'
and friendship between peoples of different countries.

But are the effects all good ones? I doubt it.
Let us look at the economic argument first. Who
are the people who actually benefit from tourism?

216

Not the mass of the people, I am sure. In fact,
very often the ordinary people are worse off because
the pressure of large numbers of tourists means that
the price of food becomes too expensive for poorer
people.

And there is another thing. Does tourism really
promote 'international understanding'? Many tourists
cannot even speak the languages of the countries
they visit. Their wealth only makes the local people
more aware of their own poverty.

My conclusion is that tourism is a harmful development and should be discouraged, not encouraged.

Exercise 8

Correct version

Extra-sensory perception

Why is it that so many scientists are reluctant
to explore the possibility of extra-sensory
perception? In the concluding chapter of his
book The Ascent of Man, Bronowski is saddened to
discover 'in the west .... a retreat from knowledge....
into extra-sensory perception and mystery'.[1] Why
should such investigation be a matter for regret?
In an earlier passage in the same book, Bronowski
admits that 'whatever fundamental units the world
is put together from, they are more delicate, more
fugitive, more startling than we can catch in the
butterfly net of our senses'.[2] It may be that science
will have to extend the range of its investigations
in order to make more significant discoveries.

---

[1] p. 437

[2] p. 364

Some useful books

Here are some books which may be useful to you in your studies:

UK background
The British Council: *How to Live in Britain* (Longman: available from The British Council, London). This booklet, which is regularly brought up to date, gives advice on all aspects of living in Britain such as insurance, clothing, accommodation etc.

Reading efficiency
Edward Fry: *Reading Faster* (Cambridge University Press, 1963). A series of easy passages for practice, with answers.
Eric and Manya de Leeuw: *Read Better, Read Faster* (Penguin Books, Harmondsworth, 1965). A much more advanced book, actually written for native speakers. Contains a lot of useful advice.

Taking notes
Tony Buzan: *Use Your Head* (BBC Publications, London, 1974). A lively, interesting book, with lots of good ideas.

Writing essays
C. J. Parsons: *Theses and Project Work* (Allen & Unwin, London, 1973). Donald J. D. Mulkerne and Gilbert Kahn: *The Term Paper: Step by Step* (Anchor Books, Doubleday & Co., New York. Revised edition 1977). Both of these books cover the whole process of writing an academic essay.
A book which gives very detailed advice on presentation is: Kate L. Turabian: *A Manual for Writers of Term Papers, Theses, and Dissertations* (University of Chicago Press, Chicago and London, 4th edition 1973).

Examinations and general study skills
Clifford Allen: *Passing Examinations* (Pan Books, London. Revised edition 1966).
Christopher Parsons: *How to Study Effectively* (Arrow Books, London, 1976). Both of these books contain very sound advice on study methods.